*British Women
Fiction Writers of the 1890s*

Twayne's English Authors Series

Herbert Sussman, Editor

TEAS 533

SARAH GRAND
The Central Library, Bath, England.

British Women Fiction Writers of the 1890s

Carolyn Christensen Nelson

West Virginia University

Twayne Publishers
An Imprint of Simon & Schuster Macmillan
New York

Prentice Hall International
London • Mexico City • New Delhi • Singapore • Sydney • Toronto

English Authors Series No. 533

British Women Fiction Writers of the 1890s
Carolyn Christensen Nelson

Twayne Publishers
An Imprint of Simon & Schuster Macmillan
1633 Broadway
New York, NY 10019-6785

Library of Congress Cataloging-in-Publication Data
Nelson, Carolyn Christensen.
    British women fiction writers of the 1890s / Carolyn Christensen Nelson
        p.   cm. — (Twayne's English authors series ; no. 533)
    Includes bibliographical references (p.).
    ISBN 0-8057-4570-X
    1. English fiction—Women authors—History and criticism.
    2. Women and literature—Great Britain—History—19th century.
    3. English fiction—19th century—History and criticism.   I. Title.
    II. Series: Twayne's English authors series ; TEAS 533.
    PR878.W6N45   1996
    823'.8099287—dc20   96-33244
                                                                    CIP

10 9 8 7 6 5 4 3 2 1

Printed in the United States of America

Table of Contents

Dedicated to my daughters, Kirsten and Heather,
New Women for the twenty-first century

Preface

Although none of the women fiction writers included in this volume is well known today, during the 1890s all of them wrote novels or short stories that achieved a wide readership. Some of their novels were even best-sellers in both England and United States. Many of these women writers became controversial figures in their time because of their willingness to deal honestly and directly with many issues affecting women's lives, such as education, marriage, childbearing, and occupations. They addressed topics that were considered unseemly for women to write about or even to know about—venereal disease, prostitution, and illegitimacy—as well as those not thought to be the usual province of women, such as religious controversies.

This book discusses the ways women writers changed the direction of the novel in the last decade of the nineteenth century by writing fiction that had a more distinctly social agenda. They created a new type of heroine who challenged conventional gender representations of woman. They also experimented with new and unusual narrative forms for fiction and were influential in the development of the short story.

By the end of the 1890s most of the fiction by these women was already out of print, and during the next century these writers were almost forgotten. Never part of the canon of late-nineteenth-century literature, their fiction has been neglected by students and scholars until recent times. Chapter 3, on the woman writer, and Chapter 8, on the critical assessment of these writers in this century, posit a variety of reasons for their brief popularity and subsequent obscurity.

The major difficulty in studying these authors today lies in obtaining copies of their books, since few have been reprinted in this century. I wish to thank the librarians at West Virginia University's Wise Library for their help in locating and obtaining materials for my study of the period.

Carolyn Christensen Nelson
Morgantown, West Virginia

Chronology

1851 Adeline Sergeant born at Ashbourne, Derbyshire, England.

Ella D'Arcy born in London.

1854 Sarah Grand (Frances Elizabeth Bellenden Clarke) born in Northern Ireland.

Mona Alison Caird born on the Isle of Wight.

1855 Ella Hepworth Dixon born in London; William Hepworth Dixon, editor of the *Athenaeum,* is her father.

Iota (Kathleen Hunt Mannington Caffyn) born in Ireland.

1856 Vernon Lee (Violet Paget) born in France.

1859 Emma Frances Brooke born in Cheshire, England.

Mary Cholmondeley born in Shropshire, England.

George Egerton (Mary Chavelita Dunne) born in Australia.

1862 Ada Leverson born in London.

1863 Mabel Emily Wotton born in Lambeth, England.

1864 First Contagious Diseases Act passed. More Contagious Diseases Acts were passed in 1866 and 1869.

1867 John Oliver Hobbes (Pearl Richards Craigie) born in Boston.

Menie Muriel Dowie born in Liverpool, England.

1868 Victoria Cross (Vivian Cory) born.

1869 Charlotte Mew born in London.

John Stuart Mill, *The Subjection of Women.*

1870 First Married Women's Property Act: established the principle that married women should in certain circumstances own and control their own property.

1871 Sarah Grand marries David Chambers McFall.

1876 Medical schools opened to women for the first time.

1877 Mona Caird marries J. Alexander Henryson-Caird.

1879 Iota marries Stephen Mannington Caffyn.

1882 Second Married Women's Property Act: married women's separate property protected.

1883 Olive Schreiner, *The Story of an African Farm*.
Mona Caird, *Whom Nature Leadeth*.

1884 Lee, *Miss Brown*.

1885 George Meredith, *Diana of the Crossways*.

1886 Repeal of the Contagious Diseases Acts.
Hobbes marries Reginald Walpole Craigie.

1888 Grand, *Ideala*.
Mona Caird's "Marriage" published in *Westminster Review*.
Egerton elopes with Henry Higginson.

1889 Ibsen's *A Doll's House* (written 1879) performed in London.
Caird, *The Wing of Azrael*.
Sergeant, *Esther Denison*.

1890 Lee, *Hauntings*.

1891 Thomas Hardy, *Tess of the D'Urbervilles*.
Henrik Ibsen's *Ghosts* (written 1881) first appears on a London stage.
Dowie, *A Girl in the Karpathians*.
Dowie marries Sir Henry Norman, a journalist and MP.
Egerton marries Egerton Clairmonte.

1892 Lee, *Vanitas*.
Sergeant, *The Story of a Penitent Soul*.
Hobbes converts to Catholicism.

1893 Grand, *The Heavenly Twins*.
Egerton, *Keynotes*.
George Gissing, *The Odd Women*.

1894 *Yellow Book* begins publication in April.
Brooke, *A Superfluous Woman*.
Caird, *The Daughters of Danaus*.
Dixon, *The Story of a Modern Woman*.
Iota, *A Yellow Aster*.

Egerton, *Discords.*

George Moore, *Esther Waters.*

1895 Oscar Wilde tried and sentenced.

Brooke, *Transition.*

Dowie, *Gallia.*

D'Arcy, *Monochromes.*

Grant Allen, *The Woman Who Did.*

Cross, *The Woman Who Didn't.*

George Moore, *The Celibates.*

Hobbes, *The Gods, Some Mortals and Lord Wickenham.*

1896 Wotton, *Day-Books.*

1897 Grand, *The Beth Book.*

Caird, *The Morality of Marriage.*

Hobbes, *The School for Saints.*

Last issue of *Yellow Book* in April.

1899 Cholmondeley, *Red Pottage.*

Sergeant converts to Catholicism.

1901 Egerton marries Reginald Golding Bright.

1903 Dowie marries Major E. A. Fitzgerald.

1904 Adeline Sergeant dies.

1906 John Oliver Hobbes dies.

1918 Representation of the People Act: certain women over the age of 30 given the vote.

1919 Sex Disqualification Act: all professions (except in the Anglican Church) opened to women.

1925 Mary Cholmondeley dies.

1926 Emma Frances Brooke dies; Iota dies.

1927 Mabel Emily Wotton dies.

1928 Charlotte Mew dies (suicide).

Representation of the People Act: all women over the age of 21 allowed to vote.

1932   Mona Caird dies; Ella Hepworth Dixon dies.

1933   Ada Leverson dies.

1935   Vernon Lee dies.

1937   Ella D'Arcy dies (date approximate).

1943   Sarah Grand dies.

1945   Menie Muriel Dowie dies.
       George Egerton dies.

1952   Victoria Cross dies.

Chapter One

Women Fiction Writers
at the Fin de Siècle

The writing of fiction by women became an essential part of the struggle for women's emancipation during the 1890s, before the movement took a more specific, political direction in the following century with agitation for women's suffrage. Excluded from the obvious sources of power in political and religious life and denied the educational and economic opportunities given to men, women used their novels and short stories to expose the limitations from which they suffered and to demonstrate the necessity for change. They created a new fiction that challenged traditional literary convention by altering the fictional representation of women's lives. Rejecting much of the gendered ideology of nineteenth-century fiction, which located women within the domestic sphere and idealized female self-sacrifice, women writers of the 1890s created heroines who broke out of traditional Victorian roles for women and who were no longer willing to sacrifice their interests for the benefit of others or to endure intolerable marriages.

Women writers created a new type of heroine, called the "New Woman," who was critical of the social conventions that hindered her personal freedom and stymied her intellectual development. This New Woman, as Sarah Grand had so aptly named her, attacked all gender-based privilege and demanded the educational and economic opportunities her brothers enjoyed. She wanted the same autonomy a man had and the chance to make real decisions about her life. Sarah Grand, along with other writers of the decade such as Mona Caird, Iota, Mary Cholmondeley, and Ella Hepworth Dixon, decried women's lack of education, which denied them opportunities for self-supporting work, forcing them into mercenary marriages. Their novels illustrated the privileging of brothers over sisters in all aspects of their upbringing and later lives.

The words "feminist" and "feminism" with their present meanings entered the vocabulary during the 1890s and were employed by critics, usually pejoratively, in their reviews of the New Woman fiction during this decade.[1] Novels before this decade were, to use Elaine Showalter's word, "feminine." Such novels imitated the "modes of the dominant tradition" and internalized "its standards of art and its views on social roles."[2] Fiction in the nineteenth century, while emphasizing the domestic role of women and their private experience, often also employed the traditional marriage plot, the narrative culminating in married domesticity.

For women writers of the 1890s, the woman problem was not that of the individual woman, as earlier Victorian fiction writers had often depicted it, but a result of flaws systemic in society. Their fiction challenged the social and economic system which deprived women of any chance for intellectual development and which narrowed the scope of every woman's life. They were especially critical of contemporary marriage, believing it no longer to be a panacea for women. Their novels abandoned the traditional marriage plot, which earlier writers used to absorb the heroine into a domestic sphere by the novel's end. Novels by New Women might begin with a marriage to reveal its problems or end with the future of the heroine uncertain. Few had happy endings in which a marriage was assured. The novels described also the lives of women who never married and the ills from which they suffered without the education or career necessary to be self-supporting.

During the 1890s women's more polemical fiction challenged conventional representations of gender roles and earlier depictions of female sexuality. These women openly confronted the sexual double standard, particularly as it related to marriage. Writers such as George Egerton portrayed women's sexual fantasies far more honestly and openly than had previous writers. Vernon Lee explored gender issues as they related to obsessional desire. Sarah Grand and Victoria Cross were the most daring in their representation of gender issues with stories of gender crossover or sexual transgression. Through their interrogation of gender roles and their portrayal of women's sexuality, women writers of the decade revealed the complexity of issues relating to gender and evidenced a sophisticated, modern understanding of sexual issues.

Not all the women fiction writers of this decade were considered New Woman writers or dealt openly with social issues specifically related to women's emancipation. Many of the short story writers, particularly Ella D'Arcy, provided a more covert indictment of conditions affecting women's lives by depicting with depressing accuracy the parasitic and distorted natures women had developed to cope with the deprivation of their lives. Their realistic stories implicitly show the same necessity for social change that the New Woman novelists had so overtly demonstrated.

The use of male narrators, particularly by the short story writers but also by religious writers such as John Oliver Hobbes and Adeline Sergeant, allowed women to explore experiences otherwise denied them, or permitted them to comment ironically on the way a woman's experience is seen from a man's point of view. The masking of female literary identity through the adoption of a male pseudonym or by the use of a male narrator also legitimized women's appropriation of traditionally male narrative techniques and literary styles. Vernon Lee's stories were influenced by the male decadent writers. Ella D'Arcy, as well as many other women who contributed to the *Yellow Book,* wrote realistic and naturalistic stories more typical of those of male writers of the time.

Other women wrote fiction about issues of general concern to both men and women in late-Victorian England. Throughout the nineteenth century novels had been published about religious conversion or loss of faith, but they were written primarily by men until the end of the century. In the 1890s, despite their exclusion from most positions in religious institutions, women wrote some of the most compelling fiction about religious experience. Narratives by women, such as Adeline Sergeant's *The Story of a Penitent Soul* and John Oliver Hobbes's *The School for Saints,* which depict doubts about traditional religious doctrines and the impact of conversion on a man's public life, significantly influenced public thinking about religious issues.

Several factors relating to the history of publication at the end of the nineteenth century contributed to this ability of women to write a new type of fiction, depict new heroines, and enter male literary territory. The three-volume novel of the Victorian period disappeared during the 1890s. The one-volume form allowed women writers more freedom to experiment with different types of fiction—shorter novels, fantasies, and short stories. The shorter, less expensive books found a growing literate audience among women, the greatest readers of fiction.

The increasing ability of private individuals to own these less expensive books broke the power of lending libraries, like Mudie's, which had tried to control the dissemination of books by banning those thought to be impure or objectionable. New publishing houses opened, among them those of John Lane and William Heinemann, which were more daring and less censorious in their policies. These publishers were willing to take risks and anxious to publish novels by women, even unknown women. Heinemann and Lane published many of the novels of the New

Woman writers, including Sarah Grand's *The Heavenly Twins* and George Egerton's *Keynotes,* as well as the Keynotes series of novels and the *Yellow Book,* both of which included many women writers.

During the 1890s the wall between popular and literary writing became less distinct. The same women who published fiction in popular magazines also wrote for literary journals. For example, while Sarah Grand's novels were being published by Heinemann, her short stories were also being published in such magazines as *Lady's Realm* and *Aunt Judy's Magazine* as well as in the *Idler.* Fiction became part of a wider public debate on gender-related social issues, which was also carried on in the popular press. One topic that moved back and forth from essays to fiction was the marriage question, with writers like Mona Caird and Sarah Grand provoking discussion by their polemical essays and through their fiction. The public responded, entering the debate with letters and essays of their own. Periodicals of the decade are filled with essays and responses to essays on the woman question. Despite the efforts by critics to enforce the boundary between popular and literary works by decrying the supposedly poor quality of women's writing, novels by women became best-sellers and their essays and stories were read by the general population.

While women writers in their fiction addressed such issues as the marriage question, the desirability of education for women, and the life of independent work for an unmarried woman, the attack against them often resulted from their frank depiction of issues relating to sexuality, including venereal disease, the sexual double standard, and the dire consequences of women's ignorance about sexual issues before marriage. Many contemporary male reviewers singled out issues relating to sex in their criticisms of women's novels. For example, a review in the *Critic* of George Egerton's *Keynotes* mentions its "suggestion of indecency," its "coarseness, commonness."[3] The objection was really not that matters of sex were being openly discussed in fiction; novels of the previous century were replete with portrayals of men's sexual adventures. But such earlier representations of sex assumed that male sexuality was natural whereas female expression of sexual desire was sinful. Now women themselves were openly writing about sexual issues, honestly depicting their own experiences and feelings.

Another objection made by contemporary critics was that these women fiction writers were presenting an ideological point of view too blatantly. Sarah Grand's novels often suffered from such criticism. The critic for the *Spectator* said that *The Beth Book* could "in no ordinary

sense of the term . . . be regarded as a novel. It is a prodigiously elaborate study of temperament merging into an impassioned and polemical
pamphlet on the marriage question."[4] When *The Heavenly Twins* was
reviewed in the *Nation,* the critic said that "the moralizing well-nigh
swamps the moral."[5] The tone of such essays, as well as their attacks on
gender-related issues in the novels, reveals that the real objection of critics was to the ideology expressed. In some cases the purpose of the novels may have been obvious, but the novels' primary fault lay in their
objectionable message.

A further line of attack was on the writing itself. Critics dismissed
many of the women's novels as poorly written and lacking in style. The
same writer who in the *Critic* found fault with Egerton's attention to
matters of sex also criticized *Keynotes* for its "utter lack of the sense of
form." He also said that "all the sketches are in the present tense and the
narrative is little more than a series of stage directions, though here and
there it is relieved by powerful sentences. . . . In a word, it is an artistic
failure" (*"Keynotes,"* 405).[6] A review of Grand's *The Heavenly Twins* calls it
"wanting in form," its polemical effectiveness "damaged by exaggeration, or, to speak more accurately, by lack of proportion."[7]

Women writers of the 1890s challenged traditional thought not only
on what should be the appropriate subject matter of fiction but also on
what should be its proper form. These women seldom wrote the tightly
plotted realistic novels that were characteristic of the fiction of most
male writers of the decade. Instead they experimented with a variety of
new techniques which allowed them to represent female experience more
accurately. For example, George Egerton uses the stream-of-consciousness method, eschewing traditional narrative to reveal women's inner
lives through dreams and fantasies. She experiments with verb tense,
often using the present to create a sense of immediacy. Many of these
writers' techniques—stream-of-consciousness, shifting points of view,
ellipsis—were employed and refined by later writers like Virginia Woolf
and became part of mainstream literature in the twentieth century.

Typical of some of the women's novels of the 1890s is their unconventional construction. These writers refused to conform to traditional
expectations for realistic and formalistic fiction. For example, Sarah
Grand's *The Heavenly Twins* does not adhere to standard formalist ideas
on what constitutes unity of plot. The narrative is interrupted after Book
4 for a complete short story that is only tangentially related to the wider
story; its connection is primarily thematic. Books 1 to 5 of the novel are
told in the third person, but Book 6 is narrated in the first person by Dr.

Galbraith, who is not developed as a major character until the novel's end. Such literary practices, seen by critics to be significant artistic lapses on the part of women writers, are now appreciated as innovative techniques. Their new fictional forms were far better able to represent the inner life of women, their shifting emotions and consciousness. The innovations these writers made in the writing of fiction actually placed them ahead of their time.

The short story became an established form by the end of the nineteenth century, in part because such women as George Egerton and Vernon Lee developed it in new and interesting ways, using it to explore the world of fantasy and subconscious desire. Women could escape the confines of their social roles by abandoning the forms of fiction that had contained them. The short story also allowed women, by breaking out of the longer novel form with its three-decker format and requisite marriage plot, to explore a new world for women that was expressed not through highly plotted action but in brief sketches and imaginative dreams.

Many popular magazines, particularly those directed toward women such as *Cosmopolitan, The Woman at Home,* and *Lady's Realm,* contained short stories written by women. Short story publication first brought many women writers to public attention. Some short story writers such as Menie Muriel Dowie became successful novelists; others, including Grand, Egerton, and Lee, published collections of their stories in book form. The *Yellow Book,* which published 13 issues during the 1890s, was the most significant literary journal of the decade for women, containing many entries by women writers; Ella D'Arcy served informally as its assistant editor.

Although portrayed by hostile critics as united by a similar agenda for social change and in revolt against established beliefs, women writers of the 1890s were never a monolithic group. Even though they pursued many common goals for women, these writers did not agree on how to achieve these goals. They shared a similar ideology, revealed in their desire to change conditions for women in England, but they disagreed on many basic issues that are still being debated within the women's movement today: Is there an essential female identity? Should marriage be requisite for childbearing? Are women morally superior to men? Nevertheless, despite the differences among these writers, they presented a united challenge to the Victorian novel. They politicized fiction, making it serve a more radical purpose than ever before. Their fiction depicted women's lives in new ways and appropriated many issues, particularly those relating to sexuality, that had long been thought to be the domain of male writers.

The demand by women for much greater inclusion in the public sphere, with its social and economic benefits, came when the door to a better life was partially opened and women could envision a more equitable world. Some beneficial changes had already taken place in the late nineteenth century, such as the passage of the Married Women's Property Acts in 1870 and 1882, and the repeal of the Contagious Diseases Acts in 1886. Women were gradually being given access to higher education with the opening of women's colleges like Newnham and Girton. In 1876 women for the first time were allowed to enter medical schools. By the last decade of the century, women saw themselves as living in a transitional period when they were beginning to realize increased opportunities but still did not enjoy the same social and economic benefits men did. Some writers like Mona Caird predicted through the voices of their heroines that the beneficiaries of their revolt would be the succeeding generations of women living in the twentieth century.

Women writers of the 1890s were in the forefront of their time in their discussion of social issues and their exploration of female psychology. Sarah Grand was the first English writer to introduce openly in popular fiction the subject of venereal disease as it related to middle-class women and to address the moral and social question of its transmission. She, as well as Mona Caird, revealed the problems married women faced in combining work and family life. Depicting a woman as musician, artist, or writer, Mona Caird, Ella Hepworth Dixon, and Sarah Grand wrote the first of the English *Kunstlerromane* with a woman as center of consciousness. George Egerton, more authentically than Freud had done, explored women's dreams and desires. These women writers were iconoclasts, challenging the accepted social and sexual roles for women. Most important, they transformed the novel by taking it out of the domestic sphere, using it to address women on issues relating to their lives and creating in it new representations of women. Their innovative literature provides the necessary transition to the fiction of the twentieth century and to the major women writers of modernism.

Chapter Two

Two New Woman Writers:
Sarah Grand and George Egerton

I. Sarah Grand: *Ideala* (1888), *The Heavenly Twins* (1893), and *The Beth Book* (1897)

In "The New Aspect of the Woman Question," an essay published in March 1894, Sarah Grand (Frances Elizabeth Clarke) wrote that the "new woman . . . has been sitting apart in silent contemplation all these years, thinking and thinking, until at last she solved the problem and proclaimed for herself what was wrong with Home-Is-the-Woman's-Sphere, and prescribed the remedy."[1] With that declaration, Grand named the new type of heroine who would dominate fiction of the 1890s the "New Woman," and proclaimed that woman's mission.

Olive Schreiner had already introduced the New Woman as a fictional heroine with her publication in 1883 of *The Story of an African Farm.* But it was Grand who named her and made her the heroine of many of her novels. Some male writers such as Grant Allen and Thomas Hardy, whose novels included New Women as heroines, were also called "New Woman writers." But the term was used most extensively to describe certain women writers of the 1890s, notably Iota, George Egerton, Mona Caird, Emma Frances Brooke, Menie Muriel Dowie, and Sarah Grand, who shared many common goals for women, although as their writings demonstrate, their means of achieving them often differed.

Grand's essay shows that the New Woman was an actual woman as well as a fictional character. This New Woman refused to be relegated to a separate sphere from men and protested against all gender-based privilege. She demanded the opportunities and freedoms her brother had, such as opportunities for a similar education and choices about whom she would marry or whether she would marry at all. In real life, the New Woman attended Newnham or Girton college, led a free and independent life, wore more rational dress, and did any number of other things, such as ride a bicycle, that seemed outside the ordinary. In fiction the New Woman was critical of the restrictive sphere to which she was confined and of present marital and economic conditions which offered her few viable choices. She was honest and open in addressing sexual matters that related to women's lives.

The gender-related social ills against which the New Woman protested are dramatically depicted in Grand's novels as well as in her essays. Much as Mona Caird used her fiction to illustrate and advance her ideas on the problems of marriage, which she simultaneously developed in her essays, so Grand incorporated into her novels many of the issues she addressed in her numerous essays. Her highly polemical novels dissolve the firm lines between fiction and nonfiction. For Grand, fiction was to serve a purpose—to change society—and to advance the causes about which she wrote and lectured.

Grand's most important novel, *The Heavenly Twins,* which developed in fiction the ideas that she espoused in her essays, became an immediate best-seller when it was published in 1893. Widely read, discussed, and attacked, the novel became part of the public debate on many issues relating to the woman question. It was also criticized on the same grounds as many other of the New Woman novels: its obvious polemics and its sexual frankness. A critic in the *Spectator* observed that "it is certain that her polemics have gone far to spoil her novel" ("Recent Novels," 395). However, the reviewer who made this charge was clearly objecting to the novel's subject matter as much as to its presentation. He claims that the questions Grand raises in the novel cannot be discussed in a journal "with a mixed clientele" (395). *The Beth Book* was also criticized for its impassioned message: "In no ordinary sense of the term can *The Beth Book* be regarded as a novel. It is a prodigiously elaborate study of temperament merging into an impassioned and polemical pamphlet on the marriage question" ("Some New," 691).

Grand would not have objected to such criticism. She intended her fiction to confront issues directly and become part of the public debate. Her novels, which were highly critical of the behavior of men, particularly their promiscuous sexuality, were sure to provoke reaction. The heroine of her first novel, *Ideala,* anticipated the next decade's hostile reviews of Grand's fiction. Ideala remarks sarcastically: "You will find that the most objectionable books are written by women—and condemned by men who lift up their voices now, as they have done from time immemorial, and insist that we should do as they say, and not as they do."[2] In an essay in the *North American Review,* Grand states that men are angry at what they are reading about themselves and rather than correct their behavior have decided that "the mirror is in fault" ("New Aspect," 276).

Grand's message on matters of sexuality, particularly on the double standard of what was considered moral behavior for men and women, was not new. Although she was criticized as revolutionary, in her call for sexual purity Grand revealed herself to be one of the more conservative of the New Woman writers. She intended that her open discussion of marriage and sexuality would lead to a higher level of general morality. But her message was presented so frankly in her essays and so explicitly in her fiction that it seemed frighteningly radical. She became associated in the minds of many of her critics with the writers of the "sex-problem novel" (Stutfield 1897, 107) simply for presenting sexual matters with a new openness as they related to women and to marriage.

Grand believed and represented in her novels that many social problems were the result of the unequal treatment of boys and girls, which was most clearly revealed in the differences in their intellectual and moral educations. A girl's interests are sacrificed to her brother's, and a boy's sense of privilege, which begins at birth, leads him to behave selfishly all his life, in utter disregard for the well-being of women. According to Grand, nothing was "expected of him in the way of virtue and self-denial."[3] Women, then, were sacrificed in marriage to dissolute and diseased men who had been raised with quite different standards of morality from women. The very ignorance and purity which women were expected to bring to marriage, and which society so valued, led them to make ill-advised marriages. The unhappy marriages that Grand saw all about her, and the miserable marriage that she herself endured for many years, caused her to view the problem of marriage as a symptom of all that was wrong with society. For her the marriage problem was inextricably linked with the woman question ("New Aspect," 276).

Accepting the widely held Victorian belief that women are morally superior to men, Grand demanded that men evolve to the same moral level as women. She believed that society was in a transitional state and could move to a higher moral level only through men's moral regeneration. But her message was primarily to women, since, Grand argued, men would not change unless women demanded that they do so and rejected husbands who did not share their standards of purity. The modern woman, she claims, wants as a husband "a man whom she can reverence and respect from end to end of his career, especially in regard to his relations with her own sex" ("The Man," 622).

Grand, along with other New Woman writers, criticized the present relationship between the sexes, especially the bleak state of marriage, in order to provoke the change required to create a better world. As a disruptive force, the New Woman would be the instrument to raise the whole tenor of society. Mr. Price, a character in *The Heavenly Twins,* articulates Grand's theory when he says: "I believe myself that all this unrest and rebellion against the old established abuses amongst women is simply an effort of nature to improve the race."[4]

The health of the nation, to Grand, meant moral and physical health, since at the time she wrote, the two were interrelated. Syphilis was rampant; for many feminists the disease and its spread became a sign both of men's immorality and of a morally diseased nation. One solution to the problem of the infection of women by men lay in women's refusing to marry dissolute men. But women could make such a decision only if they had the education to make informed choices about whom to marry and if they had some knowledge about sex before they married. Her novel *The Heavenly Twins* shows, through the experiences of two of the women—Edith and Evadne—that women's lack of education and restricted experiences prevent them from entering marriage with any knowledge about sexual diseases or their husbands' previous sexual relationships. Grand herself had little formal education, and her unhappy marriage at 16 to a man more than 20 years her senior provided her with the experiences she later gave to her fictional heroines Evadne and Beth.

Grand's novels reveal that for most women of her time, it was not possible to obtain an education that would lead to intelligent choices, particularly about marriage. None of her heroines has the education her brothers enjoy. For Grand, education for women was important, not so that they could reject marriage and have careers, which some women writers of the decade like Mona Caird desired, but so that they could make more informed choices about marriage. Grand thought that the ideal life for a woman was to be found in marriage to a good husband.[5] But in her novels none of the marriages is ideal, and few of the men could be described as good.

In both her fiction and her essays Grand combined her conservative message with a call for radical change in the behavior of men. *The Heavenly Twins* provides a severe indictment of the social approval given to dissolute men. Men, according to Grand, should aspire to the sexual purity demanded of women. She believed the alleviation of many social ills would result from the elimination of all gender-based privilege with its accompanying double standard of morality. The expectation that men bring the same unblemished past to marriage as was required of women would result in higher standards of purity. Grand very optimistically believed that with such an elevation of standards the nation would improve morally and physically.

In *Ideala, The Heavenly Twins,* and *The Beth Book*—three novels with interrelated characters who all live within a small geographical area—Sarah Grand creates many strong women characters, her New Woman heroines. Through their experiences as children and as wives, Grand is able to illustrate what she believes are the ills of society as they affect women, particularly the denial of an education to girls, which subsequently affects every aspect of their lives. Despite their best efforts, the women in these novels are unable to get the education they desire, and almost all have unhappy marriages. The latter is a result of the former: naive and uneducated women marry in ignorance about life, sexuality, and their husbands' character. They have no option other than marriage, for which they are ill-prepared. Only mere chance will give them a happy life.

The women in these novels, because of their unhappy experiences, become outspoken voices for change, most of them eventually becoming part of a group known as the New Order, women who meet to discuss social issues relating to women and who work for the betterment of women, as does Ideala. At the end of the novel of that name, Ideala pledges herself as part of that New Order to unite women across class lines in a common pursuit of change. She laments that, "Women have never yet united to use their influence steadily and all together against that of which they disapprove" (*I,* 188).

Ideala learns through her miserable marriage to a dissolute man the interrelatedness of all women's lives. The purity demanded of respectable women comes at a price to other women, who lose their respectability and are cast aside as unmarriageable because of their sexual behavior, whereas men's sexual behavior before marriage has no effect on their eligibility or respectability. Men bring a disreputable past to marriage because they have had previous sexual relationships with women who often bore their children and whom they then abandoned. Most of the men in Grand's novels have had past relationships with women whom they would never consider marrying. Ideala meets a poor girl, dying of scarlet fever, who tells Ideala that she was involved with Ideala's husband before his marriage; she calls him a "low brute" (*I,* 115) for his treatment of her. In a similar scene in *The Heavenly Twins,*

Edith meets a woman who has had a child by Edith's husband and was subsequently abandoned.

The double standard of sexual behavior for men and women is acknowledged and condoned by parents and society. Girls are kept in ignorance about all matters pertaining to sexuality before marriage, whereas boys are given license to behave as they wish with no fear of censure. Ideala includes herself in the plight of all ignorant girls: "We marry, and find we have taken upon ourselves misery, and life-long widowhood of the mind and moral nature. Do you wonder that some of us ask: Why should we keep ourselves pure if impurity is to be our bedfellow? You make us breathe corruption, and wonder that we lose our health" (*I*, 20).

The problems resulting from lack of education and the ignorance about sexuality that a girl brings to marriage are much more completely demonstrated by Grand in *The Heavenly Twins*. By tracing the development of three heroines—Edith, Evadne, and Angelica—and chronicling their marriages, Grand illustrates the devastating results of preventing girls from having any knowledge about life before marriage. One of these women, Evadne, states: "Withholding education from women was the original sin of man" (*HT,* 24). In one of her essays, Grand describes the cause and the result of women's lack of education:

> Man deprived us of all proper education and then jeered at us because we had no knowledge. He narrowed our outlook on life so that our view of it should be all distorted, and then declared that our mistaken impression of it proved us to be senseless creatures . . . and finally . . . he set himself up as a sort of a god and required us to worship him. ("New Aspect," 272)

The effects of the deprivation of knowledge are lifelong and often tragic for women. Edith Beale, the child of a bishop, is raised to believe, as many women around her—such as her mother—did, "that by ignoring the existence of sin, by refusing to obtain any knowledge of it, they somehow helped to check it" (*HT,* 156). Edith prays nightly to be kept from "all knowledge of unholy things" (*HT,* 157). When a military officer desires to marry her, and her parents despite their knowledge of his character encourage her to do so, she has no thought of inquiring about his background. Shortly after her marriage she gives birth to a deformed child with secondary syphilis. She contracts the same disease and, after suffering from brain fever and madness, dies.

The terrible price women pay for the purity of mind they bring to marriage and for society's tolerance of men's immoral behavior is graphically illustrated in Edith's suffering and death. The three men at her bedside when she is dying are her father, the bishop; her doctor, Dr. Galbraith; and her husband, Sir Mosley Menteith. Edith calls them together to impress upon them the tragedy: "to tell you, you who represent the arrangement of society which has made it possible for me and my child to be sacrificed in this way" (*HT,* 300). After Angelica, another of the novel's heroines, witnesses this scene, she takes the bishop's quarto Bible and throws it at Edith's husband, demonstrating her recognition of the church's moral failure to protect Edith or any other woman.

A realization of the complicity of the institutions of society in the destruction of women, physically and emotionally, comes to Edith on her deathbed. Evadne recognizes this collusion much earlier in her own marriage. She says: "I would stop the imposition, approved of custom, connived at by parents, made possible by the state of ignorance in which we are carefully kept—the imposition upon a girl's innocence and inexperience of a disreputable man for a husband" (*HT,* 78).

Grand was active in the movement to repeal the Contagious Diseases Acts. The passage of these acts in the 1860s made plain how the legal system blamed women for the transmission of syphilis and made men appear to be the victims of diseased women. Under these acts, women thought be to prostitutes could be seized, examined for disease, and then locked up until they were cured. Supposedly they were to blame for men's contracting the disease and spreading it to their wives. The laws also gave public acknowledgment to the fact that prostitutes were necessary so long as they were free of disease.

Sarah Grand was the first English writer to discuss openly the subject of venereal disease in fiction, particularly as it related to the lives of middle-class women, although Emma Frances Brooke's *A Superfluous Woman* (1894) also incorporates the topic into its narrative, but in a much more oblique manner. In Grand's *The Beth Book,* Beth Maclure is married to a doctor who, she learns, is the director of one of the Lock hospitals (that is, locked hospitals) to which prostitutes who were thought to have syphilis were forcibly brought and examined. When she angrily confronts her husband with the injustice of the laws and his culpability as director of a Lock hospital, she asks him, "What do you do to men who spread it [the disease]? What becomes of diseased men?" His response is, "Oh, they marry, I suppose. Anyhow, that is not my business. Doctors can't be expected to preach morals."[6] For Beth, "the iniquitous injustice and cruelty of it all made her sick" (*BB,* 401).

Far from being guardians of the nation's health, Grand's fictional doctors often are just another part of the establishment ensuring the oppression of women. Grand herself married a military doctor who was at one time in charge of a Lock hospital, and her frequent portrayal of doctors as unenlightened and unsympathetic to women must have resulted from her experience with her husband. (He was David McFall, and she had married him at the age of 16—as noted above—to escape her unhappy home.) Doctors play an important role in Grand's fiction, either as villains such as Dr. Maclure, Beth's husband, or, more rarely, as saintly men such as Dr. Galbraith who try to understand female psychology. One of the characters in *Ideala* is a doctor to whom Ideala turns for help with marital problems; he then wants her to live with him in spite of the fact that she is already married. This doctor works in a charity hospital founded for men with "mental, moral, and religious" troubles (*I,* 83); women are excluded, since "sentimentality, hysteria and silliness, [the founder] said, were at the bottom of all their mental troubles, which did not, therefore, merit serious attention" (*I,* 86). This sentiment reveals the attitude doctors often had toward the women they were supposedly treating for illness: The ailments of women are usually psychosomatic and result from their emotional instability.

The Heavenly Twins has two other heroines, Evadne and Angelica, whose lives demonstrate the difficulty of girls' obtaining an education equal to the one given boys. Both girls are highly intelligent. Evadne persists in self-education and independent reading in spite of her father's constant disparagement of women's intellectual abilities: "He was one of those men who believe emphatically that a woman should hold no opinion which is not of masculine origin" (*HT,* 5). Men held paradoxical beliefs about women's intellectual capabilities, believing that women should be denied an education because of their intellectual limitations, and yet that if given an education women might learn too much and become too independent. Ideala's question exposes this illogic: "But why not educate us to the limit of our capacity, and leave it there? Why, if we are inferior, should there be any fear of making us superior?" (*I,* 186).

Even the knowledge Evadne gains from her reading of books, including John Stuart Mill's *The Subjection of Women,* does not save her from a marriage to a dissolute military officer with a disreputable past. When she learns on her wedding day about his previous behavior, she leaves him and consents to return only if he agrees to a marriage in name only. Despite family pressure and her father's anger, Evadne refuses to sacrifice herself for her husband and to try to save his soul by attempting to regenerate him morally, which her mother and aunt believe is possible.

Such behavior on her part, she explains, would show she "is countenanc-ing vice" and "there is no past in the matter of vice. The consequences become hereditary, and continue from generation to generation" (*HT,* 79–80).

Grand repeatedly disputes the idea that female self-sacrifice accom-plishes anything beneficial for women; it merely serves to benefit men and perpetuate vice. Evadne also exposes the folly of sacrificing her inter-ests to those of her husband. She tells her aunt:

> You think I should act as women have been always advised to act in such cases, that I should sacrifice myself to save that one man's soul. I take a different view of it. I see that the world is not a bit the better for centuries of self-sacrifice on the woman's part and therefore I think it is time we tried a more effectual plan. And I propose now to sacrifice the man instead of the woman. (*HT,* 80)

Grand's rather conservative message on purity, the belief that women are essentially good and men morally debased, is articulated in Evadne's arguments with her family over the firm position she takes against any tolerance of men's immorality. But Grand makes women the agents responsible for change and addresses her message primarily to women. Men behave as they do, Grand believed, because women accept their behavior and excuse it, just as Evadne's parents did. Grand's heroine Evadne declares that she will set an example of how to change men. When her aunt advises her to forgive her husband for his past, Evadne replies, "You set a detestably bad example. So long as women like you will forgive anything, men will do anything. You have it in your power to set up a high standard of excellence for men to reach in order to have the privilege of associating with you" (*HT,* 79).

Grand's call for a new moral standard for men was part of a purity campaign that was also a component of the fiction of other women writ-ers of the 1890s, including Iota, and also of public campaigns, such as those against the Contagious Diseases Acts. The suffrage movement, in which Sarah Grand was active, later incorporated aspects of the purity ideology into its campaign, as shown by women's marching in white to represent sexual purity. According to Gillian Kersley, the Pankhursts, leaders of the more militant branch of suffragists, had an "urge to purify the male population almost as strong as their desire for the vote ('Votes for women, Chastity for men') . . . but Sarah aligned herself with the non-militant suffragists under Mrs. Fawcett."[7]

Although Grand criticizes female self-sacrifice and questions whether a woman has any obligations to a husband whom she finds morally depraved, her strong belief in the marriage bond makes her hesitant to create heroines who leave home. Despite Evadne's claim that she will not sacrifice herself for her husband, she feels unable to leave her marriage, even though it is never consummated, and she suffers within it for many years. Only after her mental and physical health deteriorate and her husband dies does she finally find a degree of happiness in marriage to Dr. Galbraith. Evadne is a heroine who survives, but she certainly does not come through her experience unscathed; she is emotionally scarred for life. Although Ideala does not go off with her doctor-lover, the novel *Ideala* presents a compelling case for divorce through her voice. Claudia, another of the women in *Ideala,* asks, "Tell me where a woman's duty to her husband ends and her duty to herself begins?" (*I,* 80).

While Edith dies of syphilis and Evadne's spirit is subdued through years of celibate marriage, Angelica, the third heroine of *The Heavenly Twins,* most clearly exemplifies the New Woman. Beginning with a paired relationship, a twin boy and girl, Grand demonstrates that many privileges are gender-related; they begin at birth and are unrelated to personal ability. Raised with her twin brother, Diavolo, to whom she is intellectually superior, Angelica refuses to have a governess and demands to study with the same tutor her brother has. Nevertheless, her rebellion achieves only limited results, since Diavolo is finally sent off to Sandhurst while she is brought out into society in preparation for marriage. To escape the constrictions of conventional married life, she takes matters into her own hands and proposes to a man who is a longtime friend and 20 years her senior. She says to him, "Marry me, *and let me do as I like*" (*HT,* 321). In her unorthodox relationship with her husband, which seems more like that of a daughter and father, Angelica gains the freedom and autonomy she desires, even to the extent of writing speeches for her husband to deliver in Parliament.

In the most daring episode in all of Grand's fiction, Angelica establishes an extramarital relationship with a young man while she is disguised as a boy. The young man, a tenor at the local cathedral who is unaware that Angelica is a woman, seemingly enjoys his relationship with her for its homoerotic overtones while she enjoys it as an extramarital affair. Through the gender confusion of this subplot, which is developed in one book within *The Heavenly Twins,* Grand interrogates the nature of gender identity as it relates to desire. No contemporary critic appears to have mentioned this subplot or found it objectionable, although the scenes of cross-dressing and exploration of same-sex love are unusual in fiction of the time.

Angelica appears again at the end of *The Beth Book,* the third and final book of Grand's three interrelated novels, as a more subdued and mature woman. An articulate and self-confident woman, Angelica, as a spokesperson for the New Order, voices Grand's optimism about the future: "This woman movement is towards the perfecting of life, not towards the disruption of it. . . . I am sure it is evolutionary. It is an effort of the race to raise itself a step higher in the scale of being" (*BB,* 412–13).

Beth, the heroine of *The Beth Book,* is also finally incorporated into the New Order, but only after years of suffering in an unhappy home and in a miserable marriage. *The Beth Book* develops many of the same ideas as *The Heavenly Twins,* such as the lifelong consequences for women of giving boys more privileges than girls. Like Evadne and Angelica, Beth Caldwell is given little education, and all the family money is spent on her brothers' education. Even her small inheritance is taken by her mother and given to her brothers. Her mother's great desire is to get Beth married as soon as possible to be rid of her as a financial burden.

One notable difference in this last of Grand's three loosely connected novels is that, unlike Edith and Evadne—the women of *The Heavenly Twins* who believe they must stay in their unhappy marriages—Beth eventually leaves her husband and becomes a published writer. Her life and career are closely patterned on those of Sarah Grand herself; Grand left her husband when the publication of *Ideala* gave her financial independence.

The Beth Book is a *Kunstlerroman,* Grand's own fictionalized life story of a writer who finds a voice for herself, just as Grand had done, first through writing, then through oratory. While still married, Beth discovers a secret attic room of her own—a private space—in which she can write, since her controlling and brutal husband discourages her writing, telling her "literature is men's work" and will make her "coarse and masculine" (*BB,* 366).

Grand's novels demonstrate how men suppress women's voices and devalue their work. In *The Heavenly Twins,* Evadne's husband makes her promise never to "join societies, make speeches, or publish books . . . on social subjects" during his lifetime (*HT,* 342). Some of the accusations against women's publications in Grand's novels mirror the very charges made against Grand and other New Woman writers. The writer Mrs. Malcomson, in the same novel, is accused of being immoral because she mentions immorality in her book. In *The Beth Book,* Alfred Pounce writes his review of Beth's book before reading it, making the usual charges against women's work:

> He condemned the book utterly from the point of view of art, and for the silly ignorance of life displayed in it, and the absurd caricatures which were supposed to be people; he ridiculed the writer for taking herself seriously; . . . he pitied her for her disappointment when she should realise where in literature her place would be; and he ended with a bitter diatribe against the works of women generally, as being pretentious, amateur, without originality, and wanting in humour. (*BB,* 517–18)

The charges Pounce makes were all familiar to Grand and to other women writers of her time. Women are condemned for their lack of artistic ability and their presumption in publishing novels. In most cases, as with Grand, what the critic really objects to is the writer's ideas, but the reviewers refuse to address those ideas.

Grand's fiction and essays gave her a public voice; women were her intended audience. Beth, Grand's fictionalized persona, said of her work, "I'm going to write for women, not for men. . . . Men entertain each other with intellectual ingenuities and Art and Style, while women are busy with the great problems of life" (*BB,* 376). Eventually Beth finds her true vocation after she leaves her husband and joins Angelica and the other independent women who had appeared in *The Heavenly Twins* and *Ideala.* She will be their spokesperson to articulate their message for changing women's lives.

Grand herself became a very popular speaker, lecturing up to 70 times a year in both England and the United States. She transformed herself from the anonymous writer of *Ideala* to Sarah Grand—her chosen name, which reveals both her rejection of the common female assumption of a male pseudonym and her strong sense of self. She did not suffer from self-doubt. Indeed, the subtitle of *The Beth Book* (which, as we have noted, is her own fictionalized life story), reads: "Being a Study of the Life of Elizabeth Caldwell Maclure, A Woman of Genius." Grand devoted her life, just as the circle of women in her novels do, to speaking for and about women in an attempt to change her society. Even though George Meredith as publisher's reader turned down *The Heavenly Twins* for Chapman and Hall, "because he found it too clogged with 'ideas,' "[8] the ideas that filled the novel resonated with women. But Grand's significance as a writer lies beyond those ideas. She is responsible for creating some of the most memorable New Woman heroines of the decade.

Evadne, Angelica, and Beth, despite all familial attempts to subdue their spirits and force them into conventional feminine roles, articulate their demands, form female alliances, and achieve some degree of happiness in their lives.

II. George Egerton: *Keynotes* (1893) and *Discords* (1894)

George Egerton (Mary Chavelita Donne) was a New Woman writer, like Sarah Grand. But whereas Grand, in keeping with her purity campaign, extolled the higher moral nature of women to which she challenged men to aspire, Egerton celebrated a woman's capacity for living a much fuller life that included freedom to express an uninhibited sexuality. Egerton looked not to Victorian England but to continental Europe for sources of inspiration. In particular, she was inspired by such Scandinavian writers as Henrik Ibsen and Knut Hamsen. In terms of style she was the most innovative of all the New Woman writers, exerting a significant influence on other writers of the decade, particularly women writers.

Egerton believed that because men and women had essentially different natures, they experienced life differently. In her essay "A Keynote to *Keynotes,*" a discussion of her first collection of short stories *Keynotes,* she states that "unless one is androgynous, one is bound to look at life through the eyes of one's sex."[9] Thus, in order to achieve authentic representations of women, women had to write their own lives. She says in that same essay, "I realised that in literature, everything had been better done by man than woman could hope to emulate. There was only one small plot left for her to tell: the *terra incognita* of herself, as she knew herself to be, as man had given himself in his writings" ("Keynote," 58). Egerton takes as her challenge that telling of women's lives. In *Keynotes* and in *Discords*—another collection of her short stories—Egerton describes a previously unexplored territory of women's interior life, their subconscious dreams and desires.

Egerton, born Mary Chavelita Dunne in 1859, was a literary unknown until the publication of *Keynotes* in 1893. Its immediate popularity prompted Egerton's publisher, John Lane, to launch a series of novels by new writers, many of them women, under the name of Keynotes. The following year, 1894, Egerton published *Discords,* which also sold well. That same year Lane brought out the first issue of the *Yellow Book,* which contained "A Lost Masterpiece," a short story by Egerton. Her inclusion in that volume put Egerton in distinguished male literary company including Henry James and George Moore. Despite the continued attacks on her by critics, who decried her frank discussion of woman's sexual nature as well as her depiction of strong, even violent, emotions, Egerton became one of the best-known and most widely read of the New Woman novelists.

Egerton drew from her own wide-ranging experiences for her fiction. She had lived in Australia, the United States, England, and Ireland. For several years she lived in Norway with Henry Higginson, a bigamist with whom she ran off in 1887 while he was married to another woman. Her realistic depiction in her stories of alcoholism and domestic violence was derived from experiences she had during the few years she spent with Higginson. His abusive behavior and alcoholic rages provided graphic and powerful material for her story "Under Northern Sky," included in *Keynotes*. Egerton's obvious relief at Higginson's death in 1889 is reflected in "An Ebb Tide," part of the longer story "Under Northern Sky," a fictional account of Higginson's last days and his death. In the story the woman returns to England with her husband's body and looks forward to "a brighter dawn" without him.[10] However, Egerton herself continued living in Norway for a while after Higginson's death, immersing herself in the literature of the Scandinavian writers, particularly Henrik Ibsen and August Strindberg. Knut Hamsen, whom she met and wrote about in her story "Now Spring Has Come" and whose novel *Hunger* she translated on her return to England, was also a significant literary influence, especially on her later writing.

Egerton's stories, which she began to write after Higginson's death and her marriage in 1891 to George Egerton Clairmonte, reveal the influence of the Scandinavian writers as well as other continental European writers on both her style and her subject matter. She shows a character's state of mind at different moments, an idea she took from Hamsen. Abandoning traditional narrative form, she creates impressionistic scenes, as in "A Cross Line," and sometimes elliptical ones, in which the motives and identities of the main characters are not clearly revealed and many details of the story are omitted. Many of her stories, for example "Gone Under," move beyond the realism of contemporary English writers, revealing the influence of the European naturalists. Egerton's naturalistic stories, like "Under Northern Sky," depict the seamy and unpleasant sides of life, creating images of desperate individuals driven to drunkenness and violence.

In some of her stories, such as "A Cross Line," Egerton employs the stream-of-consciousness technique to reveal the interior life of women, their dreams and fantasies. By this method Egerton relates what she believes to be the essential nature of women, the true feminine spirit, when it is not distorted and constricted by social forces. In dreamlike states, her female characters escape from the unpleasant realities of their lives, their loveless and often violent relationships. In "Under Northern Sky" and "An Empty Frame" women momentarily forget their husbands and become lost in dreams of movement into unrestricting spaces. Such escapes through fantasy were surely Egerton's method of coping with her experiences with Higginson and then with George Egerton Clairmonte, who proved to be as unsatisfactory a mate as Higginson had been.

Although Grand believed men and women were similar beings whose true natures were deformed by laws and social forces, Egerton posits an essentialist nature for woman which is different from man's and quite unlike its present manifestation in women. Both Grand and Egerton created New Women heroines, some of whom are able to break free from their prescribed social roles. But whereas Grand's heroines seek to create a better world by decrying the abasement of women in marriages to immoral men and calling for a higher state of morality in society, Egerton's heroines want to break free from all moral restrictions. For Egerton, such women writers as Grand, while criticizing the role society had given them as unnatural, were substituting another that was equally unnatural in that it denied their own sexuality. Egerton completely rejected the purity campaign of New Woman writers like Grand and Iota, seeing in their movement a separation of women on the basis of sexual activity into good and bad and also a denial of the inherent sexual nature of women. Her most obvious criticism of the purity school of writers occurs in her story "The Regeneration of Two" where a New Man, a sensitive poet, says of the women marching for "suffrage, purity, [and] equal wage," that "with some it was a pastime, but with most 'suppressed sex' was having its fling. . . ."[11]

In several of her stories Egerton depicts the ruinous results of men's oppression of women, whether in marriage or in any other sexual relationship, and the desperation it creates in women who can find no way out of their situation. In "Wedlock," a story whose very title intimates the sometimes grim reality of married life, a woman murders her stepchildren to get revenge on her husband, who had deprived her of her own child and the knowledge of that child's illness and death. "Wedlock" is the most extreme vision Egerton provides of the murderous violence to which women can be driven, although other stories such as "Gone Under" also portray women who have gone over the edge, or "gone under," because of their treatment by men. Elaine Showalter rightly observes that the suppressed rage of such women in Egerton's stories results from their inability to confront their real enemy, usually their husbands, because of their dependence on that person. Then they project their grievance onto an easier target (Showalter 1977, 213). In "Wedlock" the children become the targets of the woman's rage against a man. Stories such as these illustrate Egerton's understanding of the psychology of women and how their seemingly reprehensible violence is a reaction to their inability to express natural feelings.

Women's anger can also turn on other powerless individuals, such as a mother rather than the husband, as is the case in "Virgin Soil." In that story, when a young woman leaves her husband and a miserable marriage, rather than accuse him of contributing to her misery she returns to her mother to blame her for arranging her marriage, for selling her for a home, clothes, and food (*D,* 157). Marriage in the story is a contributor to the degradation of women. The daughter tells her mother: "It must be so, as long as marriage is based on such unequal terms, as long as man demands from a wife as a right, what he must sue from a mistress as a favour; until marriage becomes for many women a legal prostitution. . . ." (*D,* 155). Despite her mother's pleas, the daughter will not go back to her husband, declaring, "My life must be my own" (*D,* 154). Stories such as "Virgin Soil" and "Wedlock" are disturbing for their depictions of the grim realities of the lives of women who are powerless to change the conditions of marriage.

Egerton's heroines who have a much more benign view of marriage nevertheless still find it restrictive. Some of them are able to escape through their imaginations—their dreams and fantasies. In "An Empty Frame" a woman sleeping with her husband, whom she does not love, and thinking of a man whom she had loved and wishes she had married, "dreams that she is sitting on a fiery globe rolling away into space. . . . She seems to be sitting inside her own head, and the inside is one vast hollow" (*K,* 123). In this dream, the totality of the woman's consciousness lies within herself and she can imaginatively create her own reality.

Egerton's women find many ways and occasions to escape through the imagination. In "Under Northern Sky" a wife momentarily forgets her abusive husband when she responds to the music of a Gypsy girl outside: "What does the music rouse inside that frail frame, what parts her lips and causes her eyes to glisten and the thin nostrils to quiver?" (*K,* 147). She believes that she and the Gypsy girl, in their desire for a life of unrestricted freedom, have an affinity of spirit. The wife then falls asleep imagining she is traveling with the Gypsy girl: "The Romany lass is humming a song, a song about love, and dance, and song; and the soul of the sleeping girl floats along at her side in a dream of freedom" (*K*, 153).

The most erotic of all the fantasies of Egerton's heroines appears in "A Cross Line" where a woman imagines she is riding a horse in Arabia:

> She can see the clouds of sand swirl, and feel the swing under her of his rushing stride. Her thoughts shape themselves into a wild song, a song to her steed of flowing mane and satin skin; an uncouth rhythmical jingle with a feverish beat; a song to the untamed spirit that dwells in her. (*K*, 19)

Later she fantasizes that she is dancing on a stage before an audience moved to wonder and applause:

> She can see herself with parted lips and panting, rounded breasts, and a dancing devil in each glowing eye, sway voluptuously to the wild music that rises, now slow, now fast, now deliriously wild, seductive, intoxicating, with a human note of passion in its strain. (*K*, 20)

In her essay "A Keynote to *Keynotes*," Egerton says that although at the time she wrote these stories she was not familiar with the language of Freud and the psychoanalysts, she "did know something of complexes and inhibitions, repressions and the subconscious impulses that determine actions and reactions" ("Keynote," 58). Egerton believed that the longing for excitement and passion and for the erotic experience desired by the heroine of "A Cross Line" was shared by all women.

For Egerton, woman's true nature contained an "eternal wildness"; woman possessed an essentially "untamed primitive savage temperament" (*K*, 22). Egerton believed the Victorian representation of the woman was an artificially constructed being whose nature was distorted by the "laborious building up of moral and legal prisons based on false conceptions of sin and shame" (*K*, 40). This "untrue feminine is of man's making" (*K*, 42). The result of such distortion was a woman without a true, womanly nature. Egerton calls this woman a "hermaphrodite" (*K*, 41) and a "man-woman" (*D*, 199), while the true woman is a sensual one with a highly sexual nature. Not only was marriage often destructive of a woman's true nature and of her freedom, but it was also destructive of man's true nature. In "Now Spring Has Come," the heroine decides that "there never was a marriage yet in which one was not a loser; and it is generally the more gifted half who has to pay the heavier toll" (*K,* 64). For Egerton, any man or woman of talent chafes under the strictures of marriage, a theme to which she returns in her final story of *Discords,* "The Regeneration of Two."

While Egerton dismisses marriage as antithetical to the freedom demanded by woman's nature, she nevertheless celebrates maternity. Childbearing is for her an aspect of the essential being of women, the one element in their nature that elevates them over men. Several of her stories, such as "Wedlock," reveal the extreme reactions, even the commission of murder, of a woman deprived of her child. In "Gone Under," a woman whose illegitimate baby is killed at the direction of her lover is driven to alcoholism and a life on the streets. The friend to whom she relates her story comments, "I think the *only divine* fibre in a woman is her maternal instinct. Every good quality she has is consequent or coexistent with that" (*D,* 100). Egerton, in keeping with Darwinian thinking on the instinct for survival, believes that woman's inherent maternal desire cannot be destroyed, whether society sanctions her child's birth or declares her child illegitimate. What man has done is to create artificial categories governing a child's legitimacy in an attempt to deny women the right to create a child outside of marriage. The friend in "Gone Under" tells the despairing woman whose so-called "illegitimate" child has been destroyed that in her childbearing, "She [the mother of the child] is at heart loyal to the finest fibre of her being, the deep, underlying generic instinct, the '*mutterdrang*' " (*D,* 101).

For Egerton, a woman's desire for children is so strong that it is even capable of keeping a woman in an unpleasant marriage. In "A Cross Line," the woman decides not to run off with a lover but to stay with her husband when she realizes she is pregnant. However, childbearing without a husband is, according to Egerton, no cause for shame, even though society has made such a state shameful. As one of the women explains in "The Spell of the White Elf," " 'If one could only have a child, ma'm, without a husband or the disgrace' " (*K,* 80). The narrator of the story is subsequently, while speaking of children, so overcome by a desire for a child that she writes to a rejected suitor asking him to come to her. Whether she plans marriage is uncertain; she definitely wants him in order to have a child.

Egerton was not alone among the New Woman writers in celebrating maternity. Iota's *A Yellow Aster* also portrays a woman who is awakened to love and sexuality through childbirth. But Egerton is one of the few women writers of the decade who believed that marriage is completely unnecessary for women who wish to have children. Grant Allen had posited such a thesis in *The Woman Who Did* (1895), a novel in which his heroine Herminia Barton rejects marriage but chooses motherhood. Nevertheless, Herminia's treatment by society and her eventual suicide hardly made her decision attractive for women.

Egerton presents a far more positive picture of unmarried motherhood than did Allen. For Egerton, maternity is an innate desire whereas all legal relationships with a man are socially constructed, artificial, and unnecessary. Some of Egerton's stories, such as "The Spell of the White Elf," argue that women would be better off if they could have children without a man. Others suggest that the mother of a child would fare better without a husband. In "A Psychological Moment," the defiant woman whose reputation has been ruined says that if she had a child without a husband, she would proudly "call it mine before the whole world and tack no Mrs. to my name either" (*D*, 60).

Egerton believes that because childbearing and child rearing so dominate a woman's life—as opposed to fathering a child, which is such a fleeting experience—women have a much more important and defining role in the continuation of human life. Maternity, for Egerton, elevates and enobles women. In "The Regeneration of Two," her heroine says of woman:

> She is the flower of humanity; he, but the accessory. . . . Her maternity lifts her above him every time. Man hasn't kept the race going, the burden of centuries has lain on the women. . . . She has rocked the cradle and ruled the world, borne the sacred burden of her motherhood, carried in trust the future of the races. (*D*, 207)

Childbearing for Egerton was not a means of awakening a woman to love for a man or for recuperating her for marriage; it was something to be enjoyed as inherently feminine. To a greater extent than all the other New Woman writers, Egerton celebrates maternity and makes it women's defining experience. Shortly after the publication of these two volumes of stories, Egerton's only child, George Clairmonte, was born. She was very devoted to George, and his death in World War I in 1915 was the greatest tragedy of her life.

Just as Egerton's New Woman heroines reject the necessity of marriage for childbearing, they likewise completely defy all society's judgments of them. Egerton's most unrepentant heroine is the woman in "A Psychological Moment" who has lived with a married man and has now been abandoned by him. Knowing she is a fallen woman whom society has forever excluded from the category of respectability, she preaches to her friend defiance: "I shall apologize to no man, court no woman's friendship, simply stand by my own action, and I defy them to down me, and that is what I would teach every woman" (*D,* 61). She advises her friend to "Stand on your own feet, heed no man's opinion, no woman's scorn, if you believe you are in the right" (*D,* 64). While writers such as Grand wanted social conditions changed for the benefit of women, Egerton simply tells women to live and act as they wish and fear no one's condemnation. She empowers women to believe in themselves.

Egerton conducted her life with the same defiance she preached in her stories. She lived with one man, married two, and had numerous affairs, including one with her publisher, John Lane. From all these men Egerton took something to advance her career as a writer. From Higginson she got the experiences for her most depressing and natural-istic stories of drunkenness and violence; from George Egerton Clairmonte she took her name as a writer; and with her second husband, the drama agent and critic Reginald Golding Bright, 15 years her junior, she began her career as a writer of drama.

Egerton continued publishing collections of short stories late in the decade, including *Symphonies* (1897) and *Fantasias* (1898), as well as her semiautobiographical fiction *The Wheel of God* (1898), but none of her later work, including her drama, received the attention of *Keynotes* and *Discords*. For a few brief years in the mid-1890s Egerton exerted a pow-erful force on other writers of the decade in both subject matter and style. She also antagonized the critics and endured attacks waged on the New Woman writers, which often singled her out for special criticism. *Punch* parodied her story "A Cross Line" in several issues, calling its story "She-Notes" in imitation of "Keynotes." "She-Notes" included illustra-tions by a so-called "Mortarthurio Whiskersly," who drew mock versions of Beardsley's illustrations for Egerton's books and the Keynotes series.

More serious but no less hostile criticism was directed at Egerton in other journals. In "The Psychology of Feminism," published in 1897, Hugh Stutfield puts her works in the category of "neurotic fiction"; he argues that she writes "hysterical or squalid stories," and such writing, he believes, is not to be encouraged (Stutfield 1897, 115). Stutfield fur-ther states that "the sale of these books by thousands is not a healthy sign" (115). Nevertheless, he then acknowledges that thousands of women have written to Egerton to tell her that "there is something in us that vibrates to your touch, for we, too, are such as you describe" (Stutfield 1897, 116).

Most reviewers, even while criticizing Egerton's writing, recognize its power, just as Stutfield did. The reviewer for the *Critic* says of *Keynotes:* "It is not in its thinking, but in its force, that the book excels. A strong rendering of emotion and an acute observation rub elbows with coarseness, commonness and an utter lack of the sense of form" (*"Keynotes,"* 405). This indirect criticism of Egerton's depiction of women's sexuality as well as that directed against her unconventional style was similar to the criticism directed against Grand's writing. Often the critics linked Grand and Egerton as writers who wrote poorly as well as too explicitly about matters of sexuality.

Although her stories often reveal the seamy side of life and depict unpleasant relationships, Egerton was occasionally a utopian writer who projects a better world in which both sexes will live together harmoniously. Egerton's final story in *Discords,* "The Regeneration of Two," projects such an ideal world where women can live freely with men, without marriage, and yet fulfill themselves through work. In the story a woman opens her home to all poor, outcast women and children, who then support themselves by working together, sewing and weaving. The woman invites the man she loves to live with them without marriage. He is able to come and go as he pleases; they each pursue their individual lives. They are "free man . . . and free woman" (*D*, 251), and as such represent Egerton's ideal relationship for the sexes. The woman knows that no man can satisfy all of her emotional and intellectual needs; she requires her own work and her own independence: "She realizes well that his love, no matter if it be his whole love, will not fill her life completely; she has seen too many marriages not to know that every woman chafes at the narrowness of the horizon that is simply confined to attending to one man's needs" (*D*, 248). Egerton believed that to have a more equal relationship between the sexes men and women must allow one another total freedom. The woman in the story will forgo the "old-fashioned bondage" of marriage for a life of unrestricted freedom (*D*, 248). In "The Regeneration of Two" Egerton projects her optimistic belief in the capacity of men and women to regenerate themselves so that they can have a beautiful life unrestricted by conventions. But such a life, as most of her other stories reveal, can now only be imagined by women in their erotic dreams and escapist fantasies.

Chapter Three

The Woman Artist, Musician, and Writer: Mona Caird, Mary Cholmondeley, Ella Hepworth Dixon, Mabel Emily Wotton, and Sarah Grand

In the 1890s, for the first time, women writers made the development of creative women—writers, artists, and musicians—a subject of their fiction, writing the first English *Kunstlerromane* with women artists as the central figures. The *Kunstlerroman* with a male hero, tracing the development of the consciousness of the artist until he realizes his full talents, has a long tradition. The genre took a different direction with a woman as protagonist. The *Kunstlerroman* about a female artist is often about unrealized talent and underdeveloped artistic gifts. Recognition, if it does come, often does so at great personal cost to the woman, impairing her marriage and family life.

Mona Caird's *The Daughters of Danaus* (1894) and Ella Hepworth Dixon's *The Story of a Modern Woman* (1894) are early English examples of the female *Kunstlerroman*. The heroine of Caird's novel, Hadria Fullerton, is a musician; Dixon's Mary Erle first studies to be an artist and then becomes a writer. Many novels depicting women as writers or artists followed during the decade. Sarah Grand's *The Beth Book* (1897), published a few years after Caird's novel, chronicles the development of Beth Maclure as a writer and public speaker. Mary Cholmondeley's Hester Gresley, in *Red Pottage* (1899), is a published fiction writer, as is Valeria Du Prel in Caird's *The Daughters of Danaus*. Mabel Emily Wotton, in her story "The Fifth Edition," included in her short story collection *Day-Books* (1896), portrays the unhappy life of a woman writer, as does Ella Hepworth Dixon in *The Story of a Modern Woman*.

Although the experiences of the heroines are fictional, the problems they faced as artists were shared by their creators. The criticism leveled within the novels against fictional women writers is often remarkably similar to that being written about women writers themselves. By creating fictional women who are themselves artists and writers, women writers of the 1890s were able to demonstrate vividly, as Grand did with her semiautobiographical heroine Beth Maclure, the great difficulties that women faced in developing their talents and in fending off the hostility they provoked. Many of the obstacles they encountered were the same as those which faced women writers of previous generations, but this was the first group of writers to address the problem so openly in their fiction. Women writers of the 1890s portrayed the lives of creative women to show that the difficulties facing the woman artist were much different from and more intense than those facing her male counterpart.

Few women of the nineteenth century had careers outside the home, a woman's traditional sphere. Even by the 1890s, work considered suitable for women was limited to that which was traditionally "female," such as work as a governess. Most women who worked outside the home did so from economic necessity, and these women often were unmarried. Pursuing the life of an artist or musician or writer was not considered any more suitable for a woman than was any other work in a "man's field"; in fact it was probably less so, since it was less self-effacing. That women's work should be that which was done for others was an idea consistent with the period's idealization of female self-sacrifice. Women in their work were supposed to suppress their own identities. Obviously, writing novels, performing as a musician, or exhibiting paintings asserted the self in ways that society found objectionable. The fear that women who published would think too highly of themselves and develop an inappropriate sense of self-importance is illustrated by the remarks of Hester's brother Mr. Gresley in *Red Pottage*. Although he takes great pride in his publications, "he entreated her to join her prayers with his that she might be saved from the worship of her own talent, which had shut out the worship of God."[1]

Although women writers in the past had assumed pseudonyms, often male ones, to order to get their work published more easily or to enter male literary territory, women of the 1890s were also taking on pseudonyms, even female ones, in order to hide behind another identity, deny any ego involvement in their work, and show the proper humility required of women. Anonymity was the required trope of female modesty, the same impulse that made women of earlier generations deny they ever wanted their work published.

Of those heroines in the novels of the 1890s who did pursue the life of an artist, none is able to combine successfully marriage and family life with her artistic career. That incompatibility was shared by many actual women writers. Showalter points out that only "about 50 percent of the women writers born in the nineteenth century married; in the general population, the figure was about 85 percent" (Showalter 1977, 65). Some of the best known women writers of the nineteenth century, such as Jane Austen and the Brontës, were unmarried, or, like George Eliot, had no children, and their heroines did not pursue artistic careers.

Women writers of the 1890s were the first to give their heroines careers in the arts. The novels by women about fictional women who possessed creative ability demonstrate the difficulties married women faced in the development of their talent. The claims made upon them by their families, including parents, husbands, and children, were too consuming. Married women rarely had any private space or a room of their own in which to work. Family members constantly interrupted them and disparaged their work. The husband of Beth Maclure, in *The Beth Book,* is so intrusive in her life and so critical of her work that she finally has to write in a secret attic room. It is not until she leaves her husband that she publishes her first book.

Sarah Grand, who shared many of the experiences of her fictional heroine Beth, left her husband David McFall after the publication of her first novel, *Ideala,* gave her the financial security requisite to being independent. In an essay of 1899—"Should Married Women Follow Professions?"—Grand answers the question by discussing her own difficulties combining her duties as a married woman with her desire to write: "I tried for many years to combine housekeeping and literary pursuits, and managed both, but at infinite cost. My health, household, and literary work all suffered; and it was not until circumstances put it in my power to give myself up entirely to literature that I succeeded" ("Should," 258). Those circumstances, which she does not mention in the essay, were her financial independence and her leaving her husband. Grand ends her essay by noting that a "woman should have the same chances in the professions as a man. But a woman's work about the house is never ending . . . " ("Should," 259).

Women in fiction who wanted to pursue artistic careers also felt the claims of their family and household duties constantly upon them. Hadria Fullerton, in *The Daughters of Danaus,* seeks musical training in Paris after she marries and has children. Despite her progress with a music teacher, she eventually returns home. Her husband wants her to return, she is made aware that she has humiliated her family by leaving, and her parents' problems demand her attention. She has a great sense of guilt and of duty to others. Hadria's experience makes her realize what many women before her knew: A woman has a duty to everyone but herself. Her parents, children, and husband all claim that she is obligated to serve their needs before her own. Developing her musical talent is interpreted by her family and believed by society to be a selfish desire and certainly not appropriate for a woman who is expected to sacrifice her interests to those of her family.

The novels of the 1890s by women demonstrate the point that the unmarried woman without independent means is in an equally unenviable position if she wants to write. For financial reasons she must often live with family members. Such is Hester's fate in *Red Pottage*; she lives with her brother and his family, who are unsympathetic to her work and demanding of her time. She is made to feel that she is a burden to them. Single women who live alone, as Janet Suttaby does in Wotton's "The Fifth Edition" and Mary Erle in Ella Dixon's *The Story of a Modern Woman,* are at the mercy of their editors and publishers, because they cannot financially afford to make any demands and must give up all artistic freedom for the exigencies of the marketplace. In Wotton's story, Janet Suttaby is paid for her stories according to the number of words. She explains the demands made on her by her editor and their economic consequences: "I generally have to alter one-third, while they cut out another."[2]

Women writers were abandoning the marriage plot to write more realistically about the totality of women's lives, including the experiences of women who did not marry. However, the male editors within the fiction want women to continue to write novels that conclude with marriage and that project a happy life for women. Mary's editor, in Dixon's *The Story of a Modern Woman,* tells her that the reading public wants happy endings, which he says include weddings for women. Mary Erle is forced to alter her stories to make the endings happy. Such endings, her editor says, are what the public desires. Both Janet Suttaby and Mary Erle are extremely poor and thus cannot afford to make independent artistic decisions.

In the life of the unmarried woman writer, as it is portrayed in the fiction, work might prove to be a substitute for family and children, but not necessarily a happy one. If a woman must choose between having a family and developing her talents—and the novels imply that such a choice must be made, since no married woman can have a successful artistic career—then which is the better choice? The novels do not demonstrate that either choice is satisfactory. The unmarried writer Valeria Du Prel, in *The Daughters of Danaus,* is successful and has a wide reputation. Yet she tells her friend Hadria, who chafes against the confines of her marriage (which hinders her musical career), that her own work as a writer is not completely satisfying; it does not satisfy the heart. She fears solitude and loneliness in her old age.

The fiction by women of the decade shows that women who desire artistic careers are faced with unsatisfactory alternatives. Hadria believes that the conditions of the time make it impossible for women to make a right choice concerning marriage and a career, since the choice of one necessarily excludes the other. She tells Valeria: "It is my impression that in my life, as in the lives of most women, all roads lead to Rome. Whether one does this or that, one finds oneself in pretty much the same position at the end. It doesn't answer to rebel against the recognized condition of things, and it doesn't answer to submit."[3]

For the single woman without family, artistic creations can be a partial substitute for children. In *Red Pottage* Hester looks upon her books as her offspring, her children. When she mourns the loss of her book, which her brother burns because he believes it to be immoral, she compares her loss to losing a child, but she says her loss is even worse. A child you would see again at the resurrection, while her book is gone forever. Her novel is her spiritual child. She declares, "It was part of myself. But it was the better part. . . . I spent myself upon it. . . . I joyfully spent my health, my eyesight, my very life upon it" *(RP, 355)*. This spirit of self-sacrifice, which mothers are supposed to demonstrate for their children, Hester demonstrates for her artistic creation. She has sacrificed for her book and mourns it as a mother does a lost child.

The only solution, albeit a partial one, that any of the novels gives for the solitude of the lonely woman artist lies in the support of female friends or a community of women. Since the married woman artist receives hostility rather than encouragement from her family in the development of her talent and the single woman must pursue her vision in loneliness and poverty, the novels demonstrate that women must find the support they need in one another. Their only intellectual life lies in their interaction with other women. Hester Gresley, in *Red Pottage,* has her friend Rachel West who gives her emotional support after the loss of her novel/child. Hadria and Valeria, in *The Daughters of Danaus,* provide intellectual stimulation and personal advice for one another. Mary Erle and Alison Ives, in *The Story of a Modern Woman,* encourage each other in their work; one is an artist and a writer and the other a social worker. In Sarah Grand's novels, a group of women—the New Order, as they call themselves—meet to discuss ideas, to form a supportive intellectual community, and to plan ways to effect change. However, such alliances of women were perceived by some men to be threatening. A male reviewer of Grand's *The Beth Book* singles out these female groups for ridicule, saying they consist of "women who sit in semicircles and make speeches" which the other women then receive with applause.[4]

For their fiction, women writers drew from their own experiences— their often painful and unhappy lives—believing that their narratives would resonate with women readers. The condemnation from which their novels suffered reveals that such personal experiences were not considered genuine; or, if they were accepted as genuine, they were condemned as not significant enough for fiction. Because most women did not lead lives filled with action, these writers were criticized for having no knowledge of the world and writing from too narrow a scope. Most critics believed that men were better able to write about women's lives than were women themselves. Men's wider experiences gave them a larger vision, a more complete picture of life, enabling them to draw generalizations from the particular. In contrast, women supposedly led narrow lives, had no grand experience from which to draw, and were incapable of giving a larger meaning to experience. Criticisms such as these are reflected in contemporary reviews of women's novels. In an article in the *Quarterly Review* in 1894, William Barry said that women "cannot rise from particulars to a general view."[5]

The male impulse was to deny the validity of female experience as a subject for fiction, and then find some pathological flaw in female lives. The critic Stutfield, in an article written in 1897 for *Blackwood's,* claims that women's books "are purely subjective, or else rapid generalizations from limited experience" (Stutfield 1897, 110). After stating that many women wrote to George Egerton after her publication of *Keynotes,* telling her that she had expressed their deepest emotions and touched their lives, Stutfield remarks: "If so many hysterical people really exist, the best advice that can be given them is to try and cultivate a sense of humour and to 'bike' in moderation" (Stutfield 1897, 116). Women who wrote truthfully about sexuality in women's lives were also criticized; they were accused of creating characters who "seem to be erotomaniacs."[6]

The novels' fictional writers also are attacked for writing about a world which they did not know or understand. In Mary Cholmondeley's

Red Pottage, Hester is criticized for the novel she has published about the East End of London. Mr. Harvey, a novelist himself, questions whether she should write about a world with which he assumes she is unfamiliar. He then states: "The novel has of late been dwarfed to the scope of the young English girl . . . who writes from her imagination and not from her experience. What true art requires of us is a faithful rendering of a great experience" (*RP,* 24).

Actually Hester was writing from her experience, just as the entire novel *Red Pottage* is drawn from Cholmondeley's experiences. No matter how narrow their lives were, women writers in their novels were attacking the idea that their lives were inconsequential and did not merit artistic rendering. Cholmondeley, who led quite as constricted a life as her heroine Hester did, said about her own source for writing, "It is not my talent which has placed me where I am, but the repression of my youth, my unhappy love affair, the having to confront a hard dull life, devoid of anything I cared for intellectually, and being hampered at every turn I feebly made by constant illness."[7]

Mabel Wotton also used her own unhappy experience with male writers and editors as the basis for several of her stories and for the creation, in "The Fifth Edition" (1896), of her heroine Janet Suttaby, who writes stories that reflect the bitter loneliness of her life. While Franklyn Leyden, another writer in Wotton's story, prepares to be totally bored by the story Suttaby gives him to read and decides it has "no art about it at all" ("Fifth," 154), he is still captivated by the power and authenticity of the emotion. He believes that Suttaby has forgotten about art and has simply reproduced experience. "She had looked into her own heart, and written of what she found there, and what she wrote of was a great loneliness" (154). Leyden continues to find fault with the construction of the story, but he has to acknowledge that "it was a powerful book, because it bore so plainly the impress of truth" (155).

Women's truthful rendering of female experience challenged the expectation that women's writing should adhere to a higher moral standard than men's. Women's fiction was expected to perpetuate the idea that women did not know of sin or sex, and if they wrote about such topics, they must be of low moral character. Women writers were identified with their fictional characters far more than were male writers. Mrs. Malcomson, in Sarah Grand's *The Heavenly Twins,* learns this lesson. After she writes a book, people begin to say "that she evidently could not be moral at heart, whatever her conduct might be, because she made mention of immorality in her book" *(HT,* 334). Then one episode from the book is selected by her critics "which was most likely to damage her reputation," and readers decide it must be autobiographical *(HT,* 334).

In Cholomondeley's *Red Pottage,* Gresley believes his sister Hester is writing "trashy fiction," which the public buys to amuse itself in its idleness. He attributes her success as a writer to her pandering to the depraved public taste, then burns her second novel because he thinks that it is profane and immoral and that it will do incalculable harm if published. Equating her work with that of George Eliot, both being what he considers coarse writers, he decides that "even her good people, her heroine, have not a vestige of religion, only a sort of vague morality" *(RP,* 264). Gresley is a clergyman, and his denunciation of Hester's novel provides an interesting parallel to the reception of *Red Pottage* itself: it was denounced from a London pulpit.

Gresley's hysterical tone in addressing Hester about her writing is echoed in much contemporary criticism of women's fiction. In an essay, the critic Stutfield accuses women of writing "morbid and nasty books" whose "popularity is disquieting" (Stutfield 1895, 836). Women were blamed for the popularity of such books, since they were the greatest readers of novels. Interestingly, in condemning the novels, Stutfield reveals his real fears, fears shared by others: Women were controlling the discourse on matters that should be narrated only by men, such as discussions of sexuality in fiction. In the essay, Stutfield claims that "emancipated woman in particular loves to show her independence by dealing freely with the relations of the sexes. Hence all the prating of passion, animalism, 'the natural workings of sex,' and so forth, with which we are nauseated" (836). He selects for his condemnation novels by women, particularly novels by Iota and Menie Muriel Dowie. Then he advises boys and girls to read instead *Tom Jones* and *Roderick Random.* That recommendation makes it clear that Stutfield is opposed not to sex in fiction but rather to the gender of the person who is writing about it.

The abundance and success of novels by women during the 1890s also account for the backlash against their work. Women had usurped the role of men in their writing of fiction and in their frank discussion of sexuality in it. Women were further blamed for then reading such unpleasant novels. Lyn Pykett, discussing the anxiety created by women writers, says that "there is a constant fear that feminine feeling will erupt and invade the masculine domain of judicious impartiality."[8] The contradictions of gendered discourse on fiction, Pykett believes, are revealed in the

. . . figuring of women as both cause and cure of the New Fiction. On the one hand, women were characterised as neurotic, hysterical, morbidly introspective, slaves of the sensuous and sensual, and the producers . . . of a pathological fiction which threatened to undermine healthy, rational, male civil society. (Pykett, 43)

However, since women were supposed to be morally superior to men they were then "called upon to exercise their moral superiority and form an alliance with the philistines to discourage the production and circulation of such books" (Pykett, 43).

In the New Women's blurring of sexual lines, evidenced by their independent behavior and their co-opting of masculine territory in their development as writers, many men saw signs of cultural anarchy. There were warnings of the apocalypse; these women's fiction threatened the moral health of the country. Stutfield makes this very equation, linking women's novels to anarchism: "Along with its diseased imaginings . . . the anarchical spirit broods over all literature of the decadent and 'revolting' type. It is rebellion all along the line" (Stutfield 1895, 837–38). Then he connects the production of all this objectionable literature to a decline in manliness, to national "flabbiness and effeminacy" (843).

Clearly the threat lay in women's writing about topics that were formerly the territory of men and in their invasion and contamination of the masculine world of literature. This feminine intrusion threatened defined gender roles and made women unpleasantly masculine. That women's publication of their work disturbed many men is revealed in the objections made by male characters in the novels to women's writing. Evadne's husband, in *The Heavenly Twins,* makes her promise that she will not make speeches or publish books on social subjects during his lifetime. Beth's husband, in *The Beth Book,* tells her not to imagine that she can write, since "literature is men's work" (*BB,* 366). Women who write, he warns her, will become "coarse and masculine" (*BB,* 366).

The idea that women will become like men by writing is apparent in the many scathing comments made about the New Woman in the periodicals. *Punch* portrayed the New Women as behaving like men and disliking men.[9] Showalter rightly notes the hostility created by women's writing:

The will to write inevitably provoked some kind of hostile response, and when women had managed to resolve the conflicts between obedience and resistance, womanhood and vocation, for themselves, they discovered that they faced a critical standard that denied them both femininity and art. (Showalter 1977, 72)

Even those critics who defended the new fiction, with its more open treatment of matters of sexuality as they related to women, still believed that men were better able to write about women's lives. In an article "Sex in Fiction," published in 1895, D. H. Hannigan defends the new fiction from those wanting to censure it. In doing so, he briefly defends George Egerton's handling of sexual questions, but his primary emphasis is on male writers, such as Grant Allen. Hannigan calls Allen's novel *The Woman Who Did* (1895) "the complete history of a woman's life, and, in spite of certain faults of style and a lack of verisimilitude in isolated passages, it is one of the most remarkable novels of the nineteenth century."[10] "Men of letters" are his touchstone for greatness, and it is they who give us a "true picture of life" (Hannigan, 624–25). Here is a critic, seemingly liberal in his views, who endorses the inclusion of matters of sexuality in fiction, yet who still believes that women's sexuality is best presented by men like Grant Allen. Men should tell the story of women's lives because they do it better.

The later publication history of the fiction of these women writers of the 1890s shows how they were in many ways prophets of their own literary demise. Not only did they face hostility within their own time, but the subsequent marginalization of their work allowed men's versions of women's lives to become canonical. Women's work was denigrated and men's valorized. Thus the image of women of the period, particularly the New Woman, was memorialized as she was depicted by men such as George Gissing, Thomas Hardy, and George Moore.

A woman who wrote an unsigned essay in the *Westminster Review* in 1898 realized how women's version of their lives was already being erased by that created by men. She complained about the portrayal of women by men becoming the accepted one: "The probability is that readers of the end of this century will go on putting up with the heroines to whom the male novelist has accustomed them."[11] Her prophecy came true by the end of the decade, in that most of the fiction of the New Woman writers had gone out of print.

Women writers show an awareness of the attacks that will be made against them, anticipate them in their fictional characters, and demonstrate how they will eventually help to silence women. A male critic in Grand's *The Beth Book,* in writing a review of Beth's novel before he has even read it, makes the usual statements about women's lack of art in writing. Then "he pitied her [Beth] for her disappointment when she should realise where in literature her place would be; and he ended with a bitter diatribe against the works of women generally" (*BB*, 517–18). *The Beth Book* itself received an equally scathing review in the *Spectator* by a writer who scarcely mentions the plot but spends most of his time attacking the book's title, calling it "aggravating and strangely sounding" ("Some New," 691). While the critic within *The Beth Book* was unsuccessful in destroying Beth's novel, male critics of the time were able, through their denigration, to remove from a central position the fiction of the New Woman writers. Although the decade of the 1890s saw the publication of a great many novels in which women presented their own versions of their lives, by the end of the decade men's alternative versions had completely eclipsed them.

Men disparaged the writing of women, even their writing about their own experiences, and then usurped the tale of women's lives. Mabel Wotton's story "The Fifth Edition," describes and indicts one way this parasitic act was accomplished. Frank Leyden, a well-known writer who cannot find a new subject about which to write, takes Janet Suttaby's manuscript and publishes it as his own. Believing that men are best able to interpret women's experiences, Leyden rationalizes the deception by saying it is "the joint work of a woman dealing with the subtleties a man could not divine, and of a man writing of what a woman never notices" ("Fifth," 161). In men's writing of women's experience, he believes, "fidelity is likely to be secured" ("Fifth," 161). This story illustrates the parasitic nature of some male writers who used women's ideas and writing for their own fiction while giving no credit to the women who created it. Vernon Lee's story "Lady Tal" provides another interesting illustration of, as well as a satiric attack upon, the way a man uses his association with a woman writer to advance his own career at the expense of the woman.

Interestingly, Wotton's story "The Fifth Edition," like Lee's, is told from a man's perspective, and the dismissive attitude of Leyden toward the woman whose novel and life he appropriated is his self-revelation. Even in telling her story about losing her life and art to a man, Wotton chooses to have a man narrate the tale. This artistic decision on Wotton's part predicts the fate of women of the 1890s: Their lives are remembered as men wrote about them.

An examination of the difficulties faced by the creative women in the fiction of the 1890s and the attacks made on their work helps us understand why the women novelists themselves disappeared from the canon of the decade. Few of the novels written by women in the 1890s are in print today. By the end of the decade most were already dislodged from the canon in favor of male writers, so that today the literary representations of women's lives from this period survive primarily in the fiction of men. Women's alternative versions of their lives met the same hostility as those created by their fictional heroines. Both authors and fictive creators were denegrated by the critics and discouraged by their families in an attempt to silence them and force them to lead conventional family lives.

In Mona Caird's first novel, *Whom Nature Leadeth,* published in 1883 and quickly forgotten, Caird presented her first artistic woman heroine, Leonore Ravenhill. Leonore contemplates her approaching marriage wondering, "Could I be an artist and a wife at the same time?"[12] Doubting her ability "to attain excellence in her art" as well as "live the ordinary life of an ordinary woman" (*WNL* II, 188), she asks a friend, "Have you ever met or heard of a woman . . . becoming a real artist, or writer, or musician?" (*WNL* II, 189) The fictional Leonore never becomes a real artist, a failure experienced by the many fictional heroines of the 1890s who attempt to become successful in artistic careers. Sarah Grand's Beth is the only writer or artist or musician represented as a heroine in the fiction of the decade who successfully breaks free and fully develops her talent, and she does so only by leaving her husband and finding a group of supportive women. The other heroines—Caird's Hadria, Dixon's Mary, Cholmondeley's Hester, and Wotton's Janet— lack Beth's emotional strength and personal determination. These qualities mirror those of Sarah Grand, Beth's creator, who also left her husband to become a successful novelist and public speaker.

Chapter Four

The Marriage Question: Iota, Ella Hepworth Dixon, Menie Muriel Dowie, and Emma Frances Brooke

Most of the women fiction writers of the 1890s wrote about the marriage question. Although they used their novels to reveal the problems of marriage, to propose better marital relationships, and to examine the problems of the unmarried woman, they shared no single idea about the institution except the belief that, as presently constituted, it was not beneficial to women. What the ideal relationship for women should be elicited a variety of answers in the fiction, but despite the fears of many traditionalists, few women novelists desired the entire abolition of marriage. Views ranged from Sarah Grand's belief that the ideal life for a woman lay in marriage to George Egerton's contention that such legal ties had little relationship to women's emotional fulfillment. All agreed that marriage was in need of reform and that social reform and marital reform must proceed together, since the adverse social and economic conditions for women at the time directly affected the conditions of marriage. If women continued to be denied educational and economic opportunities, marriage for women would remain a necessity and uninformed women would continue to make unwise marital choices. Sarah Grand expressed the belief held by many women on the interrelationship between the conditions of marriage for women and the status of women generally when she wrote in an essay in 1894 that "the Woman Question is the Marriage Question" ("New Aspect," 276).

Mona Caird's essay "Marriage," which appeared in the *Westminster Review* in 1888, articulated the modern terms of the debate and involved the general public in it. After this controversial essay was published, the *Daily Telegraph* solicited letters on the topic, printing some in a daily column under the heading "Is Marriage a Failure?" The public responded with 27,000 letters during 1888, an indication of widespread interest in the marriage question, which was then being debated in fiction.

Caird's essay asserted that the problems of marriage were not individual and particular but institutional and social. For Caird, marriage as it was presently constituted was unjust to women and affected the lives of both men or women negatively. According to Caird, "the present form of marriage—exactly in proportion to its conformity with orthodox ideas—is a vexatious failure."[1] She believed marriage in her time to be a failure because women sought to marry for all the wrong reasons, which were primarily economic, since the alternative, single life, doomed them to poverty and dependency. Those who did not marry were "thrown on the world to earn their own living in the face of every discouragement" ("Marriage," 195). To Caird, such a situation had the effect of making marriage a "form of woman-purchase," since women had to sell themselves in the marriage market, a situation preferable to its alternative—economic destitution. Respectable marriages, in which the husband provided his wife with financial security and social respectability, Caird called "the worst, because the most hypocritical, form of woman purchase" ("Marriage," 195). She believed that the whole notion of respectability in women, a concept whose meaning differed dramatically when applied to men, "draws its life-blood from the degradation of womanhood in marriage and in prostitution" ("Marriage," 197). The present system is nothing more than "legalized injustice."

Caird's solution to the marriage problem lay in the economic independence of women. Women who had money or were able to make money would have real choices: to marry or not, or to leave marriages, as they desired. This independence for women could be achieved only by what she called "the co-education of the sexes" ("Marriage," 199). Caird desired that boys and girls be educated together, creating what she imagined would be a more equitable situation in which both sexes could be prepared equally for an independent life. Caird believed that people must acknowledge the evils of present social conditions that have led to the degradation of women and then refashion societal institutions for the benefit of all. She was quite hopeful that educational and economic opportunities for women would bring about a world where "men and women shall be comrades and fellow-workers as well as lovers and husbands and wives" ("Marriage," 201). Some critics agreed with Hugh Stutfield, who wrote in an article in *Blackwood's* that all such delving into the problems of marriage was a sign of a diseased imagination, a concentrating of the "attention upon whatever is foul and unlovely in life" (Stutfield 1897, 116), but most women writers saw themselves as attempting to cure a socially diseased nation by calling attention to the problems associated with marriage.

Most women writers, particularly the New Woman writers such as Iota, Sarah Grand, and Ella Hepworth Dixon, agreed with Caird that marriage was in need of reform and that the key to such reform lay in the education of women. But they did not all agree on how marriage should be reconstituted or why women should be educated. Caird wanted women to be self-supporting, pursuing careers outside the home, whereas Sarah Grand believed in the necessity of education not so much as the key to a career but as a means for making enlightened and informed choices about one's marriage partner. If women had the education men had before marriage, including a knowledge of life and sexuality, Grand believed they would choose better husbands. Thus men would be forced to raise their moral standards as they related to sexual behavior.

Another view many writers such as Grand and Dixon shared with Caird was that although the present social and economic system pitted women against one another in the marriage market and categorized them according to conventional ideas of respectability, women nevertheless shared a common experience. Their best hope for changing society lay in recognizing this commonality and in forming alliances for change. The women in Ella Dixon's novel *The Story of a Modern Woman* recognize the ties between all women and their responsiblility to one another. In three of Sarah Grand's novels—*Ideala, The Heavenly Twins,* and *The Beth Book*—women form an alliance called the New Order, which works for social changes that will benefit all women.

In her demonstration that problems of marriage were integrally tied to social and economic policies, Caird provided the groundwork for the debate on marriage that followed in the novels of the next decade. During the 1890s, novels dealing with the marriage question found a receptive audience among women, the greatest readers of novels. The marriage question became the primary topic of women fiction writers.

Despite the popularity of essays and novels by women on the marriage question, in some ways fiction by men still controlled the discourse on this issue. The best-known novel of the decade on the marriage question was written by a man, Grant Allen. In *The Woman Who Did* (1895), Allen, who imagined he was helping to emancipate women and free them from the shackles of marriage, created a heroine, Herminia Barton, who rejects marriage altogether—on principle, as a form of slavery—and has a child out of wedlock. But the novel's grim ending, in which Herminia poisons herself after her lover dies and her daughter turns against her, scarcely implies a very attractive alternative to marriage and seemingly contradicts Allen's premise about the undesirability of marriage. Nevertheless, the novel was tremendously successful, going through 19 editions in one year, and provided Allen with £100 a year in royalties until his death.[2]

Many readers believed, and some feared, that Allen's heroine was articulating the modern woman's desire to abolish marriage completely. Such was not the case, however, and many women were anxious to dissociate themselves from Allen's novel. Its publication unleashed a backlash from feminists, notably Millicent Fawcett, the well-known suffragist leader, who directed a harsh attack against Allen in the *Contemporary Review*. Allen thought his heroine was liberating herself by rejecting marriage, but many women, such as Fawcett, realized—as had Caird in her earlier essay—that the marriage problem was much larger and more complex than such a gesture would suggest. Women's place in the whole social system needed to be examined and altered; simply abolishing marriage was no immediate solution. Fawcett said that although Allen "purports to be writing in support of the enfranchisement of women," the revolution as sketched in his novel would result in "the immeasurable degradation of women."[3] His desire to abolish marriage, Fawcett believed, will benefit the "unregenerate man" and do nothing to raise the legal or social status of women (Fawcett, 629–31). Women writers of the 1890s provided in their novels more realistic possibilities about reforming marriage than had Grant.

Although many Victorian novels, such as Charlotte Brontë's *Jane Eyre* (1847) and Elizabeth Gaskell's *North and South* (1855), had used the marriage plot, incorporating the heroine into the world of domesticity at their conclusion, novels by women of the 1890s often went beyond this ending. Marriage might appear much earlier in the novel, in order to reveal its problems, or the novel might conclude with no marriage at all. The marriage plot gave way to a more open-ended development in this decade's discussion of the marriage question. What is notable about the fiction of the 1890s is the great variety of approaches taken by women to the question of marriage. Some writers demonstrated the problems resulting from women's ill-advised marriages; others portrayed what an ideal marriage relationship should be. Novels on the marriage question also described the lot of women who had expected to marry but did not.

I. Iota: *A Yellow Aster* (1894)

Iota—Kathleen (Hunt) Mannington Caffyn—one of the New Woman writers, created many independent, emancipated heroines in her novels. She possessed the same independent spirit as her fictional women, evidenced in her training as a nurse at St. Thomas's Hospital in London and in her travel, her writing, and her outdoor life. Her husband, Stephen Mannington Caffyn, a surgeon, also published fiction. Her first novel, *A Yellow Aster,* was published under the pseudonym Iota, by which she became known. Though widely condemned because of its heroine, Gwen Waring, the novel was very successful commercially, and Iota continued to create equally strong heroines in her subsequent novels.

The Yellow Aster addresses the marriage question by presenting as its heroine a seemingly radical woman who will challenge traditional ideology on feminine behavior and women's place in marriage. Gwen Waring believes that she can control her own life by selecting whom she will marry. But Iota reveals how Gwen, despite her freethinking background and independent spirit, approaches marriage with the same limitations as most other women, because the poverty of her education ensures that her only choice concerns whom to marry, not whether to marry.

By the device of pairing a brother and a sister, Gwen and Dacre Waring, and tracing their development and vastly different opportunities, Iota demonstrates that privilege is gender-related. While Dacre goes off to Eton and Sandhurst, Gwen is denied any formal education; she will stay at home until she marries. Other Victorian women writers before Iota, notably George Eliot in *The Mill on the Floss* (1860), had also paired a brother and sister to make much the same point about gender inequities. This comparison reveals that opportunity is gender-based and bears no relationship to intelligence or ability. In most Victorian novels, such as *The Mill on the Floss,* individual resistance by girls is shown to be useless in changing the conditions of their lives.

Gwen Waring exhibits a spirit of resistance despite her knowledge that she is destined for the marriage market when her brother is sent to school. She does not enter this market with the proper acquiescent spirit. She treats men heartlessly and has a "remarkably sharp" tongue and "a brutal habit of speaking truths."[4] With limited powers to effect any change in the social system, she makes her own strike against it by refusing to behave in a passive, feminine manner, instead spelling out clearly to her suitor, Humphrey Strange, her terms for marriage.

In the character of Humphrey Strange the novel mocks the pretensions of the so-called New Man who imagines that he is the modern counterpart of the New Woman. Humphrey Strange's marriage proposal to Gwen exposes the double standard for men and women in matters of sexual behavior. Strange believes he is showing that he is the New Man in revealing his past to Gwen before their marriage. He also knows that she will be "strong, and pure, and magnanimous enough to bear it." He concludes his litany of affairs with the statement, "Thank Heaven! I never loved one of these women" and then fails to recognize in Gwen's eyes her "half-triumphant interest" (*YA*, 78). Strange imagines he is enlightened because he will not hide his past from his future wife; rather, he will tell her everything before marriage. This New Man becomes a ridiculous figure in that he thinks it is fine to confess to past relationships with women he later rejects as unmarriageable. He also takes for granted the purity of the woman he will marry: that she will have no past to confess to him. The double standard of morality with its categories of pure and fallen women remains intact in his thinking despite his belief that he is a New Man who exhibits a spirit of honesty and openness to his future bride.

Gwen realizes that Strange's views on women and sexual conduct are thoroughly conventional. She will interrogate this code in her own way, by accepting a marriage proposal while freely acknowledging that she does not love her suitor. If Strange can have sex without love before marriage, and be proud of it, she will certainly have sex without love after marriage.

The novel satirizes other accepted social dogma, such as the sanctity of all childbearing within marriage, by questioning through the character of Gwen what is natural, or biologically conditioned, as opposed to what is socially prescribed. Gwen says she feels degraded being pregnant by a man she does not love, even though that man is her husband, because her condition is, according to her, "unnatural." She believes it to be more "natural" and justifiable to have children outside marriage because women in such a situation "have the excuse of love—that's natural, that purifies their shame" (*YA*, 151).

Gwen connects her own supposedly shameful situation, of being pregnant by a man she does not love even though that man is her husband, to that of the women about whom Strange had earlier told her and whom he boasted that he did not love. In Gwen's recognition of the connection between herself and all other women, fallen or pure, who bear children in what is a natural or unnatural state, Iota questions all classifications given to women which are based on their sexuality. She introduces as well a belief shared by other women writers on the marriage question: Women's lives are inextricably bound together, and the purity that some women bring to marriage is achieved only because of the so-called "fallen status" of other women.

Gwen's rebellion is not complete; it is undermined by biological impulses or maternal instincts. When Gwen gives birth, her seemingly natural instinct to love is awakened, and this love transfers from her child to her husband. Gwen's awakening to love and to her own sexuality, to feeling that "I am a woman at last, a full, complete, proper woman" (*YA,* 177), is a complete capitulation to traditional Victorian ideology, with its belief in the power of maternity to "fulfill" women and absorb them into the domestic sphere. Gwen's assertion that her femininity results from childbearing derives from the author's belief in the essentialist nature of the feminine as maternal.

The novel, which began with a radical heroine who possessed such self-confidence in her ability to control her life, ends traditionally, like many earlier Victorian novels, in a scene of loving domesticity. Even though Gwen does make choices and questions much of the gender-based ideology of her time on marriage, she cannot assert her independence against the claims of biological determinism. Whether Iota was unable to project Gwen's rebellion beyond motherhood or whether, as she said of her novel, it was "her aim to show that motherhood will awaken the heart of even the most insensible woman,"[5] the novel depicts Gwen's rebellion as limited and subverted through that which is maternal.

The title of the novel is derived from Gwen's belief that she is unusual, as is a yellow aster. It most likely also derives from the decade's vogue for the color yellow; the novel was published in 1894, the same year the *Yellow Book* first appeared. According to Holbrook Jackson, "Yellow became the color of the hour, the symbol of the time-spirit. It was associated with all that was bizarre and queer in art and life, with all that was outrageously modern."[6] Iota's use of that color in her title was most certainly advantageous to the novel's sales, but it also made readers link her and her heroine to the decadent and modern.

However, Gwen is in no sense one of the decadents, and although she begins as a modern New Woman in her rebellion against prescribed feminine behavior, the novel fails to deliver the promise of its title or of its heroine. Nevertheless, Gwen's initial rebellion against the artificial constraints of traditional marriage may be evidence of their unnaturalness, just as her eventual submission to domesticity through maternity appears to be natural, or biologically determined. Although other writers, most notably George Egerton, also believed in the essentialist nature of woman revealed through her maternal instinct, Iota, unlike Egerton, uses this instinct, the biological imperative of childbirth, to recover a woman for her traditional domestic role.

II. Ella Hepworth Dixon:
The Story of a Modern Woman (1894)

When Mona Caird argued in her essay "Marriage" that women choose marriage because the alternative is a life of grinding poverty as a single woman, she was accurately assessing the plight of Ella Dixon's heroine Mary Erle in *The Story of a Modern Woman.* Mary begins her life fully expecting to marry Vincent Hemming, but when he abandons her for a wealthier woman, she joins the world of work—for which she is ill prepared because of her lack of formal education. The death of a father at an early age, struggles as a writer, and single life are all reminiscent of Ella Dixon's own life as well as the life of her fictional creation, Mary. Dixon's treatment of the marriage question in this her only novel becomes an examination of the lives of those women who had expected to marry but did not, as Dixon herself did not.

In the latter half of the nineteenth century, England had a supposed surplus of women: The population of women far outnumbered that of men. By 1901, this surplus exceeded 1 million in England and Wales.[7] Many women had no expectation of ever marrying, and some women, agitating for the education of women as Mona Caird did, used this statistical fact as further reason to demand that they be given the same educational and economic opportunities as men, since many women by necessity would have to be self-supporting. These unmarried women were the "odd," or "leftover," women about whom George Gissing wrote in his novel *The Odd Women* (1893). They often led lonely, poverty-stricken lives. By contrast, the single man, both in literature and in life, was never seen as a problem. In fact, he was often a dashing and enviable figure, whereas the very label given to the woman, "odd," revealed that she was a type who did not fit into the social and economic system of the time.

Mary Erle, Dixon's heroine, joins the ranks of these odd women even though she is far better off socially and economically than most. After her father's death, she enrolls in the Central London School of Art, hoping to get into the Academy and thus become successful enough to earn her living as an artist. But in her struggles and failures in the world of art, Mary learns much about the plight of working women, a group with whom she now identifies, despite class differences, as she never identified before.

Dixon's great achievement in this novel is to create two women characters, Mary Erle and her friend Alison Ives, who see their lives as connected to those of women of all classes to whom they have a responsibility. Right after her father's death, Mary notices the seamstress in the house, sewing alone, doing monotonous work, accepting her servility. Then "an immense pity seized her for the patient figure . . . the figure of the woman at her monotonous toil."[8] Mary has several such epiphanies in the novel in which she experiences a sudden identification with suffering women. Her friend Alison also identifies directly with poor young women, her "East-end girls" (*Story,* 40) as she calls them, to whom she is devoting her time. She desires "to be in sympathy with her own sex" (*Story,* 39).

Both Mary and Alison experience the betrayal of trust by a man. In a hospital Alison meets a woman who is the abandoned lover of the man she intends to marry. That woman's suffering prompts Alison to ask Mary, "Promise me that you will never, never do anything to hurt another woman. . . . If women only used their power in the right way! If we were only united we could lead the world" (*Story,* 213). In the face of men's abandonment of women, of their destruction of women's lives and respectability, and in their labeling of woman as a "social evil" (as Alison's male lover had labeled the poor woman he deserted), women must find solidarity with one another and demand from men "ethical standards of conduct" (*Story,* 216). This call for greater purity in men, and for women to ally themselves with one another in demanding such purity, reflects Grand's message in many of her novels.

The two women in this novel share the belief that by working together women can help change society, but neither expects to benefit from any such change in her lifetime. Remembering Alison's advice, Mary rejects Hemming, although she still loves him, when he returns to her to ask her to run off with him while he is still married. She tells him, "I can't, I won't, deliberately injure another woman. Think how she would suffer! . . . All we modern women mean to help each other now" (*Story,* 255). Mary makes a commitment to the solidarity of women and to their support for one another because of the trauma she experienced when Hemming left her for another woman and because of the suffering she has witnessed in other women's lives. She connects the helplessness of her own lot with all women's generally, even with that of Hemming's wife, her supposed rival.

Even though society has pitted women against one another and made them rivals in a marriage market, Mary and Alison refuse to see other women as competitors. They recognize that the real enemy is the man-made social system, with its different expectations of sexual conduct for men and women—expectations that made some women ineligible for respectable marriage while making other women the seeming beneficiaries of such injustice. This hypocrisy in the relationships between men and women is destructive of the lives of Mary and Alison, as it was of the lives of other women in the novel.

Like many other Victorian novels, *The Story of a Modern Woman* pairs the experiences of a brother and sister to reveal privilege that is solely gender-based. Mary has a brother whom she supports in spite of her poverty. He goes to Winchester and Oxford, getting the education to which he is supposedly entitled by his class and gender, while Mary, suffering financially, turns to writing to support herself.

The public does not desire to know the realities of poor women's lives. Mary finds this out when she writes a novel and her editor rebukes her for making the ending far too grim; she must make it happy, since the public demands happy endings in fiction. "The British public doesn't expect them [the novels] to be like life," the editor explains (*Story*, 182). The women need to be happily married. The disparity between the fictional the world of the women she is creating and the reality of her own lonely existence is painfully apparent to Mary. Although she can change the ending of her novel to suit her editor, she cannot change the conditions of her life—given the existing social and economic situation.

Dixon does not give us the happy ending Mary's editor had demanded of her. After Mary rejects Hemming's offer to run off with him and writes the "happy ending, the rapturous *finale* which the public demanded" (*Story*, 267), she climbs the road to visit her father's grave at Highgate Cemetery. Despite the "joyous activity of spring-time" all around her, Mary knows her life will be a sad and lonely one: "Henceforward she was to stand alone, to fight the dreary battle of life unaided" (*Story*, 270).

As the title of Dixon's novel indicates, Mary is a type, one example among thousands of women who are forced to work and face the future alone with little preparation for such a life. The novel depicts the loneliness and poverty single women faced in attempting to make their way in a world that was created by and for men and in a society where women are seemingly powerless to control their own lives.

Dixon's novel demonstates that the marriage question—which, as Sarah Grand had said, is linked to the woman question—must also take into account those women who never marry, the odd women such as Mary, who suffer "in a world of artificial laws; of laws made for man's convenience and pleasure, not for [theirs]" (*Story*, 264–65). Dixon's solution to the problem is the one which Alison articulates to Mary and which Alison demonstrates through her actions in the novel: Women must unite by joining with one another in solidarity across class lines. Therein lies their only hope for social change and for the creation of a new world of possibility for unmarried women such as Alison and Mary, and even Dixon herself.

III. Menie Muriel Dowie: *Gallia* (1895)

Gallia Hamesthwaite, the heroine of Menie Muriel Dowie's *Gallia*, has an Oxford education, and this, according to Caird's and Grand's beliefs, should cause her to fare better than most women when making decisions about marriage. But she finds her path to marriage difficult when, as a New Woman, she acts on her liberated philosophy about sexual relationships while at the same time still being judged by a society that defines gender roles very traditionally. Gallia is a rational and outspoken woman living in a world where innocence, ignorance, and beauty are considered by men to be female charms. Although she recognizes this reality, Gallia never wavers in her faith that total honesty is the best course to pursue in her dealings with men.

Gallia did not grow up playing with dolls or studying music. Instead, she learned three languages, studied natural science, and read John Stuart Mill and Herbert Spencer before going to Oxford. The men about her were looking for cheerful, mindless women to marry, but Gallia's "eyes were clouded with wonder upon wonder about matters which have strained the strongest and toughest brains the world has ever seen."[9] Conceding that her intelligence puts Gallia too far head of her time, Dowie observes early in the novel that "there are a great many Gallias in the world now-a-days, and they are, for the most part, very unhappy people" (*G,* 68).

Dowie's portrayal of her heroine is both sympathetic and comic. Gallia's actions, which result from her uncompromising ideals and her unwillingness to make any concessions to contemporary notions of propriety, often result in humorous situations. When Gallia tells her Oxford friend Dark Essex that she loves him, because she wants to be completely honest about her feelings even though they are not reciprocated, he asks, "Don't you think the world is still a little too raw for your very advanced treatment of it?" (*G*, 101). Gallia disagrees: Although she may be misunderstood or disliked, she finds "no excuse for not acting in accordance with the light one has" (*G*, 101). Such sentiments put into practice make Gallia both admirable and, at times, rather foolish.

The variety of women in the novel—mistresses, prostitutes, traditional wives and mothers, naive young women, cynical social climbers—represent all the types who had their place in a Victorian society permeated with hypocrisy and deceit about men's relationships to women. Men knew which of these women were marriageable and which were best kept hidden. Gallia upsets all the convenient ways of thinking about women and the methods used to navigate the marriage market. Applying rational principles, she will choose a man herself and her choice will be based on the laws of eugenics in order that she can have a strong, healthy child. Gallia decides that who fathers her child is of far more importance than whom she marries and that the two men need not be the same person. The desire to be a mother and to love one's child, Gallia says, is innate in women and far more satisfying than marriage. She believes that "a woman gets a great deal out of motherhood; more than she does out of marriage" (*G*, 156). Gallia joins the list of heroines of the decade, including those in the fiction of George Egerton and Iota, who celebrate maternity above all other instincts in a woman.

Gallia's ideas may seem sensible and rational to her, but they shock her Oxford friend Dark Essex, who was the former object of her affection. He reacts to Gallia's pronouncements as would most men of his time. When she says that she no longer cares about love, that she does "not comprehend the emotional kind of happiness to be got out of some man's admiration of me . . . [and that] love did not seem to me a happy thing" (*G*, 213), he responds by telling her that she is "the perfectly hapless kind of modern woman . . . [and that] there is no place in the world for you. You are not wanted, because you are for no use" (*G*, 214). He finally labels her a "misshapen woman" (*G*, 215). Such criticism might prove devastating to most women, but Gallia's self-confidence is undisturbed by Dark's rejection of her ideas. She "knew the scorn was not his, but was his outraged sex speaking in him" (*G*, 215).

In her complete lack of concern for social convention and her total honesty with men—to the point of telling the man whose proposal she accepts that she does not love him but has simply selected him as husband because she wants him to father her child—Gallia almost becomes a caricature of the New Woman. The novel's brittle wit results from Gallia's practicing the most advanced ideas concerning marriage and maternity on an unprepared world which would rather perpetuate its hypocritical practices concerning sexual relations. For example, when Mark Gurdon's marriage proposal includes the obligatory confession of past affairs, Gallia talks about his mistress with total approval; she finds nothing in his past that needs forgiveness. Furthermore, if she doesn't love Mark, how can she possibly be jealous of other women?

Gallia, in her denial of all sentimentality and physical desire, is perhaps an exaggeration of the New Woman, but despite the author's earlier warning that such women are unhappy Dowie nevertheless creates for her a measure of joy. Gallia does not succumb to neuroses or early death, unlike other heroines who are too advanced for their time. Neither does she ever completely give up her ideals. She agrees to marry, but on her terms, being totally honest about not loving Mark. Gallia hints that when she is alone with him she will yield to impulses of desire, but at the same time claims that she is not acting according to her feelings and that "all the dead women in the world who have done identical things at such moments are coercing me, are pushing and constraining me to act as they did" (*G*, 312). Just as Iota's Gwen finally responds to love for biological reasons, Gallia believes that she also must succumb to the impulse to procreate. But Gallia never loses her independent spirit the way Gwen does. When her husband asks, "Can't you see what a lovely thing it is, this sweet instinct in women—in all good, true women—to respond to, and to love the man who loves them," Gallia replies, "No, Mark, I *can't* see it—I never could see it" (*G*, 313). The idea that women before her are urging her to acquiesce and respond to Mark provides Gallia with a good biological justification for acting on sexual feeling. She is aroused not by a man but by generations of women before her who urge her to respond to him: "the dead women of the world were having their will of her, were triumphing in her" (*G*, 315). They will ensure that she fulfills her longing to be a mother.

The novel's ending is somewhat comic, in keeping with its tone throughout, which is much lighter than that of most women's novels about marriage during the 1890s. Gallia's aunt, Mrs. Leighton, optimistically hopes that Gallia will eventually fall in love with Mark. Dark, whose hereditary heart disease is proof that he doesn't fit into Gallia's eugenics plan and that she was right in not marrying him, is sent off to dispose of Mark's mistress. The reader is left wondering whether the discarded mistresses also found happiness. The New Woman, despite her unconventional thinking, has dismissed them too easily in her pursuit of the ideal man to father her perfect child. Nevertheless a novel on marriage published in 1895 which ends with two happy marriages—one that is conventional and one that is not—and no unhappy ones is certainly a notable literary event. Few other heroines of the 1890s had a good education, chose their own husbands, set the terms for marriage, or lived happily as did Gallia.

Gallia was considered one of the more shocking of the New Woman novels because its heroine chooses her husband in such a calculating way, on eugenic principles. Dowie herself anticipated the response the novel would receive, in a scene within the novel. Through Gallia, she expresses the anxieties of women writers of the decade concerning the reception of their radical ideas. Urged to write down her ideas on eugenics, Gallia declares that the publication of her ideas would only group her with others leading the sexual revolt, and thus she would not be taken seriously. Reminded that much attention is now being paid to what women write, Gallia responds, "What they say makes so much noise that nobody hears properly what it is. A woman who really feels these things shouldn't write about them now, until what they call the boom of women is over" (*G*, 195).

Gallia is too far ahead of her time to provoke rational discussion of her ideas or to find a sufficient challenge to her theories on eugenics. Her ideas shock women and are dismissed by men as neurotic or simply "curious." To some, she is a "misshapen" woman, as Dark Essex calls her; to others, she is an oddity. Nevertheless, she is greatly attractive both in her physical beauty and in her unusual frankness. Gallia may be cheerfully eccentric, but her idea of improving the world through principles of selective breeding would be controversial at any time.

Dowie, who divorced and remarried, disregarded public opinion in her own life as did Gallia. She did not heed the warning not to publish which Gallia voices but continued to publish novels and also write stories for the *Yellow Book*. Her first book, *A Girl in the Karpathians* [sic], has as its heroine a great traveler like herself who dresses like a man. Nevertheless, the remarks Gallia makes about the "boom of women" reveal Dowie's awareness that women's novels of revolt, including her own, were all being thrown together by critics and not taken seriously. They were considered a passing phenomenon. As a friend advises Gallia, a woman must publish her ideas under a man's name in order to be taken seriously, to which Gallia responds, "Men don't think these things" (*G,* 195). Dowie used her own name to publish one of the most humorous of the New Woman novels on marriage to appear during the 1890s.

IV. Emma Frances Brooke: *A Superfluous Woman* (1894) and *Transition* (1895)

Emma Frances Brooke's *A Superfluous Woman* was one of the best-selling of the New Woman novels when it was published anonymously in 1894. The novel employs Brooke's socialist agenda to engage women's issues, particularly on the marriage question, which for Brooke could not be addressed without a discussion of the evils of the class system in England. A member of the Fabian Society from its inception in 1884, Brooke lived at different times among socialist groups that supported themselves through manual labor. She believed that individual happiness could be found only in a life of work and that inherited wealth was destructive of both individual and national health.

Brooke's novels deal with both gender and class privilege, and for Brooke both are equally reprehensible. In *A Superfluous Woman,* disease is indicative of aristocratic degeneracy and a metaphor for the many ills, usually class-related, from which society suffers. The heroine, Jessamine Halliday, the "superfluous woman" of the title, is an idle woman of the upper classes who suffers from an illness brought on, according to her doctor—who functions as a spokesperson for Brooke throughout the novel—"by ennui and excessive high breeding."[10] Because she serves no useful purpose in society, the only way she can regain health is through a rejection of her class privilege and through physical labor.

Jessamine regains her physical health when she flees the life of London society to live in Scotland as a laborer. There she falls in love with a noble farmer who is unaware of her origins. In this pastoral episode Brooke gives us a socialist vision of the ideal life in which men and women labor physically side by side. Such a life of shared labor, Brooke believed, erases class and gender distinctions.

The novel could have ended quite happily, with Jessamine and the farmer marrying, but Brooke reveals the lasting effects on the personality of one's early life. Jessamine has been permanently infected with diseased ideas relating to her class, from which she can never entirely free herself. She persists in thinking of herself as socially superior to Colin, the farmer.

Brooke links the simple life of manual labor to all that is natural and to a person's true nature, whereas the life of London society is associated with all that is artificial. That which is natural also manifests itself in spontaneous physical passion, as demonstrated by Colin, which Jessamine fears and to which she cannot completely respond. The artificial upbringing Jessamine has experienced has permanently destroyed her ability to respond to the natural. Her eventual return to London is a rejection of the uninhibited sexuality and economic austerity which Colin offers her.

The man Jessamine marries, Lord Heriot, is also physically diseased, even more so than she. Brooke's portrayal of Heriot illustrates her belief that disease is inherited by the aristocracy as a manifestation of class privilege and a life of idleness and dissipation. Heriot is debauched, alcoholic, and probably syphilitic, and his family all suffer from these same problems, which Brooke shows are passed down as the nobleman's inheritance from a long line of degenerate men. He has a drunken brother, an idiot sister, and a paralytic father. Their physical degeneracy is a manifestation of their moral and social diseases, both of which are caused by their privileged position in the class system. Over time the family has "degenerated into meanness, irritation, and vice" or "insanity, disease, and shocking malformation" (*SW,* 277). The children Jessamine bears by Heriot, an idiot girl and a deformed boy, eventually destroy one another in a vicious fight. The doctor who visits the family and shares Brooke's view of the aristocracy as degenerate believes that Heriot's "race should pass into annihilation" without an heir (*SW,* 284). This wish is fulfilled when the unborn baby dies and Jessamine deteriorates into madness, perhaps from syphilis, and dies herself.

Brooke was not the first writer to equate physical and moral disease. Ibsen had introduced the idea of a morally degenerate lifestyle contributing to hereditary disease in *Ghosts,* which first appeared on the London stage in 1891. Venereal disease, or its literary representation, is also an important issue in Grand's novels, particularly in *The Heavenly Twins,* where it is presented as an indication of men's immoral behavior which infects and destroys women's lives. Elaine Showalter, in *Cultural Anarchy,* points out that "the syphilitic male became an archvillain of feminist protest fiction, a carrier of contamination and madness, and a threat to the spiritual evolution of the race."[11] In her novel, Brooke widens the scope of the moral implications of disease beyond Grand's; she believes disease to be a sign of degeneracy as it relates to issues of class as well as gender. However, both Brooke and Grand belong to the "purity school" of New Woman writers in their attitude toward moral degeneracy. Equating sexual purity with moral purity, such writers believed that men should live by the same restrictive sexual code demanded of women, since it represented a higher level of morality.

Although *A Superfluous Woman* became Brooke's best-known work, *Transition*, published a year later, in 1895, "By the author of *A Superfluous Woman*," is much more successful in combining Brooke's feminist agenda with her message of salvation through socialism. The heroine of *Transition*, Honora Kemball, an intelligent, well-educated woman, is far more engaging than Jessamine. Honora successfully combines a life of useful work, a passionate love for a man whom she will marry, and a socialist worldview. She may very well be the first New Woman heroine to "have it all" without compromise.

Transition makes literary use of Brooke's activities as part of the Hampstead Historic Society, the Fabian group of which Brooke was secretary. In their course of study during the winter of 1887–1888, various members of the group presented papers on such topics as the utopian socialists, the Chartists, and the Positivists. A year later this group included as one of the subjects of its study the women's movement.[12] Out of this study came many of the ideas and characters of Brooke's novel. In *Transition* Honora's father, a clergyman, is converted to Chartism under the influence of a poor parishioner, a former Chartist, and much to Honora's initial dismay, her father decides to lead a life of poverty. Rejecting such a life as her father has chosen and desiring to make use of her Girton education, Honora goes to London, where she falls under the influence of various socialists, particularly Leslie Littleton, whom she eventually marries.

Honora is an educated and independent woman, much like Brooke herself, who was educated at Newnham College, Cambridge, and was also connected with the London School of Economics. Just as Brooke had, Honora finds satisfaction and even happiness in her life of work. She tells Littleton that her work completely satisfies her, her independence suits her, and she will never marry.[13] But then a moment of "great and golden glory of passion . . . came to her" and she tells Littleton: "I have great need of love" (*T,* 330). With that the novel ends.

Brooke, who never married herself, ends her novel quite traditionally with a projected marriage. She brings together her feminist heroine and her idealist reformer, both of whom champion Brooke's own socialist vision for transforming society through physical labor and economic equality. Just like Iota's heroine Gwen, Brooke's Honora responds finally to biological impulses that awaken passion. Honora is incorporated into marriage but, unlike Iota's heroine, she is an independent woman in an equal partnership with her own life of work.

Brooke, like the other Fabians, had an optimistic view of an emerging utopian future, as people work toward the gradual breakdown of class and gender distinctions. While *A Superfluous Woman* shows a failed attempt to achieve that goal and a disastrous marriage, *Transition* concludes on a happy note. Honora and Littleton will work together, just as Caird in her essay on marriage in 1888 had suggested would be possible if women were educated with men. Caird spoke of a world where "men and women shall be comrades and fellow-workers as well as lovers and husbands and wives" ("Marriage," 201). Brooke projects such gender equality for her heroine at the end of her novel. *Transition* is one of the few novels of the decade to provide such an optimistic answer to the marriage question.

Chapter Five

Novels of Religious Doubt and Faith: Adeline Sergeant and John Oliver Hobbes

By the late nineteenth century women were writing some of the most widely read religious novels. The century had produced many novels of religious experience; these works depicted contemporary challenges to the established church generated by evangelicalism, the Oxford Movement, and Darwinism. Fiction became one vehicle by which writers with a variety of different beliefs could enter the debate on religious issues. Some writers used their fiction to convert readers to their religious positions. Others, such as J. A. Froude in *The Nemesis of Faith* (1849), used the novel to tell the story of their loss of faith. John Henry Newman's *Loss and Gain* (1848), the story of a young man's attraction and conversion to Roman Catholicism, is close to being an intellectual debate, an analogue of the education at Oxford of Charles Reding, the novel's protagonist. In such conversion narratives by men, religious conflicts became intellectual problems, requiring a reasoned response, and later in the century the literature by men also reflected the aesthetic appeal of High Church religion.

Women too wrote novels during the nineteenth century that revealed contemporary religious anxieties, but seldom do their fictional characters directly discuss religious doctrines. Because women were excluded from orders in both the Anglican and the Roman Catholic churches as well as from the universities where much of the religious debate took place, fiction provided them with an opportunity to inject their opinions on religious experience into the public arena. But women wrote from a different perspective than men. They were outsiders influenced by the ideas of the religious debate, and yet were never afforded the opportunity to actively participate in it. Thus women's religious novels, including conversion narratives, seldom presented religious conflict as an intellectual experience as Newman had done. Instead, religious belief was a matter of the heart, often relating to a love interest. Such well-known writers as

Charlotte Brontë, in *Villette* (1853), and Mary Ward, in *Helbeck of Bannisdale* (1898), created Protestant heroines whose attraction to Catholicism derives from their romantic interest in Catholic men. In her novel *The Vicar of Wrexhill* (1837), Frances Trollope, mother of Anthony and herself a much published novelist, reveals her antievangelicalism by exposing the duplicity of a clergyman, an evangelical within the Church of England, who tries to seduce a rich widow. Women writers such as these portrayed their female characters as being susceptible through their emotions to religious conversion.

Women in the 1890s entered the religious debate, but on their own terms. To widen the scope of their religious fiction, giving it a greater social and political impact than the mere story of a woman's attraction to a lover of another religion, Adeline Sergeant and John Oliver Hobbes centered their religious narratives written during the 1890s on the lives of men who have public roles, either in the church or in political life, depicting the religious doubts and conversion experiences of male protagonists. Neither writer in her fiction directly indicted the established church for its marginalization of women. But by their dramatization of the religious experiences of men, whose faith and conversion have important public implications, these writers revealed how small a role women played in religious and public life. Conditions for women being what they were, novels about religious doubt and faith could not be as significant when centered on a woman's life, since the woman's actions would have few implications beyond the personal.

In the religious novels of both Sergeant and Hobbes, a love interest remains an important component of the religious experience of both male protagonists. The men in their novels have their religious faith tested by a variety of means, the most important resulting from their attraction to deeply religious married women. By presenting male characters whose personal lives affect their religious and public lives and by making a romantic interest an aspect of religious attraction, Sergeant and Hobbes are able to create narratives of broad appeal.

Adeline Sergeant and John Oliver Hobbes, who experienced many of the same religious uncertainties as their male protagonists, began life as Protestants and died as Catholics. The Oxford Movement, Darwinism, and the dissenting sects, all of which raised important challenges to the doctrines of the Church of England and were of male origin, found their way into these women's novels. But the challenges represented in their novels are to the faith of men; the women are peripheral figures just as they were in the Church of England and the Roman Catholic Church in Victorian times.

I. Adeline Sergeant: *The Story of a Penitent Soul* (1892)

One alternative to traditional religious belief in the last half of the nineteenth century was faith in science, particularly a belief in progress leading to the social and physical improvement of human beings—an idea seemingly justified by the determinism Darwinism exerted on religious thinking in the later nineteenth century. Adeline (Emily Frances) Sergeant's *The Story of a Penitent Soul* demonstrates the dramatic effect Darwin's ideas of determinism had on religious thinking in the nineteenth century, and the failure of science to provide moral certainties after eroding religious faith. For Stephen Dart, the protagonist of the novel, the seemingly antithetical answers given to his questions by religion and science are equally deterministic and ultimately unsatisfactory. By the end of his life, Dart believes that "the testimony of the modern scientist was as conclusive as that of Calvin. We are as our ancestors have made us. We act and believe as we do because of our environment. . . . What amount of individuality has any one of us? Our environment is our Fate."[1] The determinism or lack of free will inherent in religion and science, at least in Calvinism and Darwinism, leads Stephen to a despairing conclusion about his own ability to act freely and control his own behavior. Although he had rejected the doctrines of his uncle, a Methodist clergyman, who had impressed Stephen with the idea that he has bad blood in him which will surely manifest itself, the events of Stephen's life partially confirm that deterministic belief. His behavior provides evidence that science is right in its theory of biological inheritance.

The Story of a Penitent Soul is presented in the form of a journal written at the end of his life by Dart, a dissenting minister who has left the church but has not entirely lost all faith. Dart is the illegitimate son of a woman he had been raised to believe was his aunt. As a child and unaware of his so-called "bad blood" (which his uncle believes is a result of his illegitimacy), Stephen aspires to become a Methodist clergyman like the uncle who has raised him. But his religious confusion begins early in life. As a boy he reads the works of such pious writers as Thomas à Kempis and George Herbert but, he says, "while drawing all my religious inspiration from the writing of a Roman monk and an Anglican priest, I had an intense horror of the Churches of England and of Rome alike" (*Soul,* 24). Stephen's first religious confusion begins after he enters training to become a Methodist minister. Upon his mother's death his uncle tells him the truth about his illegitimate birth. In shock over such news, he leaves the school he has been attending and begins work for Dr. Egerton, who espouses "liberal and advanced views" (*Soul,* 108), those of a universalist. In embracing a new message, the "good tidings of purity, peace and love" (*Soul,* 117), a more humanistic religion, Stephen believes he has taken up the beliefs of some of the most advanced thinkers of his day, among them Harriet Martineau and Matthew Arnold, who ignore religious doctrine but embrace morality. He then accepts a call to an independent church.

Through Stephen's two friends and advisors the author offers quite different antidotes for Stephen's religious problems: on the one hand, science with its denial of the reality of sin and, at the other extreme, religious enthusiasm with its message of rescue from sin. Allan Herrick, Stephen's lifelong friend and a successful doctor, presents to Stephen the scientific view "that there was no such thing as sin in its theological sense; that wrong and criminal acts simply indicated disease, or an inherited tendency" (*Soul,* 135). Such a view of sin is of no comfort to Stephen, because he believes that if sin is an inherited tendency, it is also inescapable. But at Allan's recommendation, Stephen begins to read Darwin, Huxley, and Spencer. Allan's faith in only that which he can see, his rejection of the idea of sin, and his belief that man is not responsible for his imperfection, all directly challenge Stephen's great desire to believe in some divine being who can rescue him from the circumstances of his supposedly disreputable birth. Stephen's other friend, Charles Egerton, the son of Stephen's mentor Dr. Egerton, takes another path, becoming a "fervent evangelistic preacher" (*Soul,* 231). Rejecting Egerton's religious enthusiasm, Stephen nevertheless adopts his social message and, at Egerton's suggestion, begins to spend time helping the poor in his parish, seeking salvation through altruism.

The many changes Stephen undergoes, his variety of religious beliefs, and his search for something in which to place his faith are similar to the experiences of many Victorians, including those of the author. Although Adeline Sergeant began life as a Methodist, she became an Anglican, a Fabian, and in 1899 a Catholic. Another of Sergeant's novels, *No Saint* (1886), was written during the brief period of her agnosticism, and *The Story of a Penitent Soul,* published in 1892, reflects several phases of her religious life, particularly her attraction to dissenting sects and to socialism, but not her final Catholic phase. The ambivalence of this novel's ending reflects Sergeant's own uncertainty about which religious direction she will take.

Stephen Dart does not end his life as an agnostic, but he comes perilously close to it. He resigns from his church, saying he will never accept another call. His action is precipitated by an affair he has with a married woman from his church. The relationship is discovered by her husband when she gives birth to Stephen's son. The parallels between Stephen's own birth and that of his son, both occurring outside of marriage, reinforce Stephen's belief in hereditary determinism, whether it results from biology or from religion. He believes that he must have inherited his father's nature.

The belief that immoral behavior can manifest itself as physical disease which then can be transmitted from one generation to another is illustrated in the fiction of contemporary women writers of the so-called "purity school," such as Sarah Grand and Emma Frances Brooke. The growing popularity of the eugenics movement, with its desire to apply Darwinian ideas of inheritance to the biological improvement of the human species through selective breeding, informs *Gallia*. In Sergeant's novel, Dart discovers his father "is dying of diseases which he has brought upon himself by excess" (*Soul*, 182), suggesting venereal disease. At the novel's end Stephen and his son are both physically weak and as a result will appropriately, according to Darwinian ideas, die without heirs.

In explaining to himself the similarities between his behavior and that of his father, Stephen transposes the language of science to that of religion: He must be predestined to eternal damnation because of his evil father and sinful birth. Being foreordained to sin, as Calvinism would teach, is for Stephen no different from being biologically determined to evil by one's ancestors, as some interpreters of Darwin would have it. Stephen finally asserts his need to believe in a God who will help him escape the chains of heredity—whether they derive from science or religion: "The doctrine of heredity, as laid down by some writers of our time, and assimilated vaguely by innumerable readers, is a stumblingblock of many; and I believe that there is no way of surmounting it but by a firm grasp on the supernatural" (*Soul*, 292). But he is still filled with doubt and can only hope there is a higher being.

Stephen's final religious position closely resembles that of Alfred, Lord Tennyson at various moments in his elegy *In Memoriam*. Stephen longs for faith but suffers from doubt. He masks his doubt in speaking to his dying son, reassuring him that they will meet in the afterlife. But to himself he admits, "If I could but think that you and your mother would not watch [for me in the afterlife] in vain!" (*Soul,* 298). He asks God to "forgive these words," these "tears for all that I have lost" (299). Such words recall Tennyson's own lines, coming after moments of religious doubt, partly evoked by evidence from evolution, "Forgive these wild and wandering cries." Matthew Arnold's "Dover Beach," which asserts the value of human love in a time of unbelief, is also echoed in an earlier scene of Sergeant's novel, when Stephen visits the ocean with his lover and listens to the "long withdrawal of the wave" (*Soul,* 188), believing this brief moment with his lover to be one containing both sweetness and pain.

By her creation of a male protagonist, Sergeant can illustrate problems of faith through the experiences of a clergyman, a public figure. But like earlier women writers, she introduces a romantic attraction to test religious belief. Stephen is sexually attracted to a seemingly unattainable woman. But his love interest compounds his religious confusion, the same problematic role love played in Charlotte Brontë's *Villette* and Mary Ward's *Helbeck of Bannisdale,* novels centered on women's experience. Stephen's attraction to Mary Fleming, the woman he loves, reflects his religious and sexual confusion. Stephen loves Mary for her purity while desiring her physically. He says she reminds him of a Madonna he has seen in a picture in her "passionlessness and sweetness" (*Soul,* 150), and at the same time he feels a strong sexual attraction to her. When Stephen willingly sells his soul for the ecstasy of the passionate moment he has with Mary, his religious convictions pale in comparison with his biological sexual drive.

Sergeant does not draw Mary as a complete woman; her almost total passivity throughout the novel—she asserts herself only when she confesses her affair to her husband—makes her appear less culpable in the relationship than Stephen. But that passivity also detracts from any intellectual attributes she may have. She finally wills her own death, unable to resolve her conflict over her illicit love for Stephen and her fear of damnation. Mary's desire to die is the ultimate act of self-effacement, female self-sacrifice in its most extreme form. There is no satisfactory place for her as an adulterous woman in society or in the church. Mary's experience reveals how few categories exist for women within religion as it was practiced—they can only be pure or fallen—and how small a place is given to women's sexuality in a patriarchal religion.

While all Mary's religious doubts result from her affair, Stephen suffers from religious confusion throughout his life. The peace he sought as a child in repeated religious conversions, and as an adult in science, social work, and sexual expression, is never permanently attainable.

The anguished debate over religious questions dramatized in Sergeant's novel is similar to that which took place within Sergeant herself. Her father, like Stephen and his uncle, was a Methodist clergyman; she did not leave that church until after her father's death.

II. John Oliver Hobbes: *The School for Saints* (1897)

John Oliver Hobbes (Pearl Mary-Theresa Richards Craigie), a better-known writer than Sergeant, is the most important English Catholic novelist of the 1890s. Her brief, miserable marriage to Reginald Walpole Craigie, an alcoholic philanderer who may have infected her with venereal disease, provided her with material for some of her fiction. Many of her novels, such as her very successful *Some Emotions and a Moral* (1891), are written with the cynicism and wit that characterized the mood of the decade and are not about religious issues. But the novels for which she is best known today deal with Catholicism and with the personal and political consequences conversion to that religion had for her protagonist. In 1892, two years after leaving her husband, Hobbes (whose family were Congregationalists) converted to Catholicism. Her Catholic novels, *The School for Saints* (1897) and its sequel *Robert Orange* (1900), reflect her own commitment to Catholicism but reveal also the attendant difficulties of conversion to that faith for a man seeking public office in Protestant England. Her final novel, *The Dream and the Business* (1906), depicts the clash between Nonconformists and Catholics—the two religions to which she was at different times an adherent.

While Adeline Sergeant's hero experiences his religious conflict in the context of the religious doubt generated by the climate of Victorian England, Hobbes's hero in *The School for Saints,* Robert Orange, struggles on a much larger stage. His religious experience and conversion have an impact on his public life and are played out against the political life of England and the rebellious conflicts of continental Europe in the 1860s. His last name links him unmistakably with Irish Protestant history; even the word "orange" had long been anathema to Catholics. Hobbes's novel, with its large scope and great number of characters, some of them actual political leaders of the time, reads like historical fiction but is set only 30 years before publication.

Like Sergeant, Hobbes uses a male protagonist to dramatize the author's own religious conflicts. Also like Sergeant, she merges her religious fiction with the female tradition of religious novels by including a love interest. Men in the fiction of both Sergeant and Hobbes are attracted to married women of devout faith. In the case of Robert Orange, who begins life as a Protestant, the attraction to Catholicism comes in many ways, but his love for and lifelong devotion to Brigit Parflete, a Catholic and a married woman, is definitely an important factor. (Her name may hint at that impulsive medieval saint, Birgitta of Sweden.) Similarly, Robert's father, who had been a monk in the Order of St. Dominic and had abruptly left the order to marry Robert's Protestant mother, let passionate desire for a woman guide his religious decisions.

The attraction to Catholicism, intellectual for many men influenced by the Oxford Movement and, later in the century, sensual for the aesthetes, is presented here as emotional—linked to romantic desire. Robert Orange's attraction to Roman Catholicism, which combines the female interest in emotion with the intellectual interests of earlier protagonists in male religious writing, is also presented as an attraction to a more sensual religion than that of the Church of England. Mary Ward's novel *Helbeck of Bannisdale,* published one year later than Hobbes's, also reveals this desire for a religion of greater sensuality, which Ward also combines with romantic desire. This attraction reflects the interrelationship between the High Church movement and aestheticism in late Victorian England. Catholic ceremonies and sacraments appeal to Robert's emotional nature and his capacity for intense feeling. Initially, though, the very sensuality of the Catholic religious experience makes Robert fear and distrust this sacramental religion. He says, "I cannot allow myself to think that ceremonies which bring such a glow of unspeakable, inhuman happiness can be intrinsically right or pleasing to God. It is an intoxication of the soul."[2]

Robert's artistic and sensual nature makes him reject a life of priestly celibacy. He is strongly attracted to Brigit, a very young woman who is married right out of a convent, whose marriage is unconsummated, and who repeatedly flees to various convents for safety. Robert's love for a chaste Madonna figure is similar to that of Sergeant's Stephen Dart, whose lover is said to resemble a Madonna in a painting. Robert Orange's Brigit is a figure of perpetual chastity—even Robert's eventual marriage to her is never consummated. Robert visits the convent where Brigit is living because he is greatly attracted by her physical beauty, but he is also enticed by the "nuns' pure, almost unearthly voices singing the beautiful Litany of Loreto" (*School,* 495). But in Hobbes's novel as well as in

Ward's, Catholicism has another side, a call to asceticism. One recalls that Robert Orange's father was the monk and later the lover who flees the monastery for physical passion.

The linking of sensuous beauty with the chaste life of the convent embodies the paradoxical appeal of Catholicism, with its attraction to both the physical and the spiritual nature of an individual, depicted in the novels of other nineteenth-century women, notably Charlotte Brontë and Mary Ward. Although these earlier writers used women as protagonists, Hobbes's novel recasts that female religious experience of the heart using a male protagonist. Religious conversion for Robert Orange is an experience primarily of the heart and secondarily of the mind, but it contains conflicting and contradictory impulses.

By providing her story with a large setting and giving it national and political implications, Hobbes extends the boundaries of religious fiction beyond those given it by most women writers. Robert Orange's attraction to Catholicism and desire for conversion are set in the context of the political life of England in the late 1860s, when religious choices were sometimes made for reasons of expediency. When Robert runs for a seat in the House of Commons, he is warned for political reasons against conversion to Catholicism by the novel's fictional version of Benjamin Disraeli (1804–1881), himself a Jew whose conversion to the Church of England allowed him eventually to become prime minister: "I must warn you that such a step would prejudice your whole political career" (*School*, 115). Disraeli urges compromise between Rome and Canterbury, declaring "that the best-ordered life is that which shows the largest record of compromises" (*School*, 113). That advice, which served Disraeli well politically, Robert rejects. He converts to Catholicism and runs for office in 1869. Although he is pelted with garbage and called a Jesuit, he narrowly wins a seat.

Hobbes's interest in Catholicism as it applies to European politics is a significant part of her novel. Her creation of a protagonist whose name is Orange and who converts to Catholicism reveals a desire on her part for a return to Catholicism in England. Robert, as part of a group of English men and women whose goals are religious as well as political, becomes involved in the Carlist cause, an attempt to restore the Bourbon monarchy to Spain. He travels to Spain with Lord Wight, who is carrying with him a miniature of Mary Stuart and an "unfinished essay on the iniquities of Elizabeth" (*School*, 238). While Robert himself becomes a partisan only inadvertently in an attempt to restore Don Carlos as king, he nevertheless imagines "France and Spain united under one King and forming one great Catholic power" (*School,* 378). The Carlist cause is both Catholic and monarchist; therein lies its attraction for Robert. It is also an anachronistic cause that is certainly doomed to failure.

Hobbes reveals her own sense of being part of a marginalized and at times despised religion by representing her hero, Robert Orange, as a man of great faith and principle who suffers for his religion in his public life, in both England and Spain. His employer, Lord Reckage, dismisses Orange as his secretary on learning of his conversion to Catholicism. He faces harassment from the electorate when running for office, and he is physically injured and then ridiculed for his involvement in a losing monarchist cause.

Although *The School for Saints* has over 500 pages, the novel does not complete the full life story of Robert Orange; rather, it ends with his marriage to Brigit. Another novel, *Robert Orange* (1900), completes the story of Robert: He separates from his wife after her husband is found to be still alive, and then he becomes a priest. Robert's marriage with Brigit was never consummated, just as hers to Parflete had not been. The celibate husband and his virginal bride are romanticized and para- doxical figures. In a most untraditional way, Hobbes is thus able to write a novel using the traditional marriage plot yet reconciling it with the ideal of purity through sexual chastity in both her male and her female protagonists.

Hobbes's own experiences are reflected in the ambivalence of her hero Robert Orange toward sexuality. After her divorce Hobbes became involved with several men, the most notable being the novelist George Moore. They became literary collaborators, writing a play, *The Fool's Hour,* a witty drawing-room comedy that appeared in the first volume of the *Yellow Book* (April 1894). Although some critics, such as John Sutherland (300), have suggested that Moore and Hobbes's relationship was both literary and sexual, others believe she "opted for Catholic chastity" for the rest of her life (Todd, 330). Moore's unflattering fic- tional presentation of Hobbes in "Mildred Lawson," a novella in his book *Celibates* (1895), implies that his relationship with her was never sexual. In Moore's story, Mildred Lawson is a heartless woman who finally pleads, after a lifetime of rejecting men, "Give me a passion for God or man, but give me a passion."[3] The relationship between Moore and Hobbes, always tempestuous, deteriorated, and Moore got his revenge on Hobbes by re-creating her as a fictional woman who could not truly love anyone, God or man.

Hobbes's conversion to Catholicism appears to have had no adverse effects on her literary career, perhaps because as a woman she was in no danger of involving herself in religious or political affairs. Nevertheless, her family was horrified by her conversion. Hobbes had always had a strained relationship with her mother: The constant conflicts between the two led to several suicide attempts by Hobbes, and her death at an early age was rumored to have been by her own hand.

Paradoxically, the novels of conversion by Hobbes and Sergeant gave women writers the influential and intellectual voice in the religious debate that was denied their fictional women characters. Through their male protagonists, these writers demonstrated many of the challenges to religious faith and some of the enticements to conversion they themselves experienced. They created complex male characters whose romantic interests played an integral role in their religious conflict. But they did not solve the problem that any woman novelist of religious fiction faced: how to make female characters develop as interesting and complex figures when women played such peripheral roles in the life of most churches. Nevertheless, judged by their popularity, the religious novels of Sergeant and Hobbes, like those by other women of late-nineteenth-century England, had a broad appeal for both men and women and even attracted readers who were not caught up in religious controversy.

Chapter Six

Vernon Lee and the Short Story

The literature of the 1890s that was most disruptive of gender categories and most unsettling to bourgeois values was written by the New Woman writers and by the decadents, including such writers as Oscar Wilde and Ernest Dowson. Some mainstream writers, such as George Moore and George Gissing, also wrote literature that had decadent overtones. Although both groups of writers—the New Women and the decadents—were often attacked by critics as if they shared a common agenda, there were clear distinctions between them, particularly in their quite different representations of women.

The stories Vernon Lee (Violet Paget) wrote during the 1890s do not reflect the feminist ideology, with its demands for social change, that was prominent during the decade in much of the work of women writers, particularly the New Woman writers. Neither do most of Lee's stories employ the realism and naturalism typical of many of the short stories written by women. Instead, her work reveals the influence of the male decadents in its representation of gender "slippage" and its preoccupation with "perverse" women characters.

Born Violet Paget in France in 1856, Lee spent most of her life outside England, primarily in Italy. Thus she was not affected by the same restrictive social climate as were women in England. Her stories, almost always set on the continent, demonstrate that her interests centered less on social conditions than on psychological states, particularly as they relate to desire. Although during her lifetime Lee was known chiefly for her historical studies, aesthetic criticism, travel literature, and drama rather than for her fiction,[1] during the 1890s she published two collections of stories, *Hauntings: Fantastic Stories* (1890) and *Vanitas: Polite Stories* (1892). These stories are important for their exploration of erotically charged psychological obsessions and their scathing portraits of narcissistic men.

All the stories in *Hauntings* are about the fascination that a contemporary character, usually male, has for a character from the past. Invariably, this character becomes so obsessed with the historic one that he loses all interest in the present and willingly accepts death as a means of uniting with the object of desire. For the obsessional character, the imagined world, with its highly charged erotic attractiveness, overshadows and consumes the present reality through the power of sexuality.

Lee's stories of obsession bring together actual historic and fictive characters, both mythological and contemporary. Indeed, this mingling of fact and fiction was precisely what the publisher Blackwood objected to in rejecting her novel of the title "Medea da Carpi" which later became the story "Amour Dure," the first of the stories in *Hauntings*.[2] This story is told through the diary entries, over a period of four months in 1885, of Spiridion Trepka, a Polish professor from Germany. While doing research on the history of Urbania, Italy, Trepka learns of Medea da Carpi, a woman who had lived in the area 300 years before. Like the classical Medea, this Medea's life was filled with violence. Men in the past supposedly were tortured and killed for her. Fascinated rather than repelled by her life, Trepka excuses Medea's actions; he sympathizes with her in her imprisonment and regrets her early death at age 27. Finally he falls madly in love with her, despite his realization that in so doing he would soon die, as had all her previous lovers.

Increasingly the events of the story take on a sense of unreality, so that the real and the imagined merge in Trepka's mind and in the reader's. Trepka begins to see Medea, she writes him letters, and he becomes obsessed with her. Then he justifies his actions, which were done at her instigation: "The love of such a woman is enough, and is fatal—'Amour Dure,' as the device [her necklace] says. I shall die also."[3] Trepka realizes he may be delusional in his fantasy about Medea and in his belief that he is able to see her and communicate with her. Nevertheless, he does actually die for her, though the identity of the person who kills him remains a mystery.

Because Lee's stories are often told from a limited point of view, such as through one person's letters or diaries, they create an indeterminacy that makes it difficult to distinguish between events which actually occur and those which are created by the narrator's imagination. In "Amour Dure," the narrator's various sightings of Medea appear to take place not in the actual geographical sites to which he refers but in his fanciful imagination. We never know who kills Trepka, whether Medea returns to murder him or someone else does so or whether he kills himself for love of her. Also mysterious—and inexplicable—is Trepka's love for such a violent and heartless woman. Is she a beautiful woman come to inspire in him an unearthly love, or is she the destructive witch others think her to be? The many ambiguities of Lee's stories provoke multiple interpretations, the same effect Henry James achieved in *The Turn of the Screw.* The delusions that fascinate and haunt the fictional characters also disturb the reader through their multiplicity of suggestion.

In "Dionea," Lee demonstrates through a male narrator and a male protagonist the power of the mind to create a femme fatale of such over-powering attractiveness that a man will die for her. The events of "Dionea" are recounted through a series of letters from an Italian doctor to a princess. A sculptor in Genoa becomes obsessed with a girl, Dionea, whom he uses as his model for a statue of Venus. Her origins are unknown by the villagers because she had been washed up on shore as a child, but she seems to be a goddess, displaced from ancient Greece into the modern world. Her decidedly pagan nature, her ability to cause people all around her to fall in love, her distinctive behavior—such as lying under myrtle bushes—and her extraordinary beauty identify her as Venus. But the dances of the villagers that Dionea inspires and the final sacrifice the sculptor makes to her, as well as her name, also recall the myth of Dionysus. Many local men are strongly attracted to Dionea, but the sculptor's interest in the girl becomes overwhelming. He finds her beauty far surpasses that which he can artistically create. He then sets up his studio on the former site of a temple of Venus. While viewing Dionea's uncovered body as he attempts to reproduce it in art, he is driven to a murderous frenzy, finally sacrificing his wife on an altar of Venus before committing suicide. Dionea is last seen sailing off on a Greek boat singing, with a myrtle wreath on her head.

In "Oke of Okehurst," Lee presents another artist figure. He is painting the portrait of Alice Oke, a woman he calls the "most graceful and exquisite" (*H*, 123) he has ever seen. This artist, while revealing his own obsession with Alice Oke, narrates the story of her obsession with a long-dead ancestor, also named Alice Oke, with whom she begins to identify. The earlier Alice had supposedly been a conspirator with her husband in the murder of her own lover. The husband of the present Alice—believing that he is seeing Lovelock, the earlier Alice's lover, and that Lovelock is involved with his wife—shoots his wife and then himself. The portrait painter, who is living with the Okes while painting Alice's picture, is never able to complete his painting of her. He cannot satisfactorily represent her great, unearthly beauty on a canvas.

In Lee's stories in *Hauntings,* the modern world cannot provide the exquisite beauty and passionate love that can be found by imaginatively entering a past world and joining a historic person. Trepka is aware that no earthly woman can offer what Medea possesses: Only the imagination can capture that which reality cannot provide, just as the artists' rendering of their subjects, in both "Oke of Okehurst" and "Dionea," continually falls short of the imagined ideal.

The blending of obsessional desire with eroticism, evident in "Amour Dure," "Oke of Okehurst" and "Dionea," is most fully developed in "A Wicked Voice," a story in which a composer cannot write his opera because he keeps hearing the voice of an eighteenth-century singer, Balthasar Cesari, known as Zaffirino. The proud Zaffirino had boasted that no woman could resist his singing: It would drive her mad with love and cause her to die. While discounting this story as foolish, the composer himself falls under Zaffirino's spell. He is both attracted and repelled by the voice but also by the portrait of Zaffirino's face, with its decidedly effeminate appearance. While looking at the portrait he says: "I have seen faces like this, if not in real life, at least in my boyish romantic dreams, when I read Swinburne and Baudelaire, the faces of wicked, vindictive women . . . and his voice must have had the same sort of beauty and the same expression of wickedness" (*H,* 206). The composer is trying to write the harmonies appropriate to a Scandinavian legend, but he finds them "strangely interwoven with voluptuous phrases and florid cadences in which I seemed to hear again that same accursed voice" (*H,* 216). He calls the voice "accursed" while still acknowledging "that this voice was what I cared most for in all the wide world" (*H,* 234). The voice is indeed wicked, because it causes him to lose his inspiration to compose.

Like the other stories in this volume, "A Wicked Voice" is about an attraction to a historic or mythic time and person that is so compelling that everyday reality pales in comparison. But in all the stories the fascination with the person from the past contains elements of the sensual, and the pursuit of the erotic experience is linked to a desire for death. In the first three stories of *Hauntings* the desire is to possess a fascinating but unattainable person. The result of this obsession is death. In "A Wicked Voice," the composer longs to hear the voluptuous music of Zaffirino with its overtones of decadence and forbidden love; he suffers, not death, but the loss of his own creative inspiration.

"A Wicked Voice," like the other stories in *Hauntings,* blurs gender lines; its gender crossovers give it homoerotic overtones. Although the voice the narrator hears belongs to a man, it sounds much like a woman's (it is probably a castrato's), and the evil that he finds in Zaffirino's voice and face are distinctly female, derived from his nightmares and dreams about wicked women but transposed onto an eighteenth-century man. Gender confusion is reinforced when the male narrator finds himself in the situation of the women who had previously become entranced by Zaffirino's music and fallen under his spell.

Most women writers in the 1890s rejected men's representation of women and female sexuality. George Egerton, who depicted women's sexuality in her fiction most overtly of all women writers of the decade, presented women's sexual fantasies and dreams of uninhibited self-expression. But Egerton showed these imaginings from a woman's point of view, as a woman wishes to behave and to be desired. By contrast, Lee narrates all her stories in *Hauntings* and *Vanitas* either through men or from a male character's point of view. They are primarily about male desire or female desire as described by a man. Lee's female characters are highly eroticized fantasy figures of male desire in stories narrated by men.

With the exception of "A Wicked Voice," these stories narrate experiences of obsession with women who are dangerous, often violent figures who move outside acceptable female boundaries. Even in "A Wicked Voice" the voice and face of a man become imaginatively transformed into images of wicked women. These women are the femmes fatales found in male decadent literature, women as they are both desired and feared by men. Their displacement from the distant past or from the realm of mythology into contemporary life makes them dangerously disruptive but sexually attractive as well. Additionally, Lee adopts a male persona for herself as writer through her use of a male pseudonym, a name partially taken from her half-brother Eugene Lee-Hamilton. Lee's narrative method distances the reader from the women characters and renders them figures of a male imagination, femmes fatales of dangerous destructiveness. The several layers of male identity Lee assumes contribute to the gender confusions and tensions of her stories, particularly "Dionea" and "A Wicked Voice." Telling her stories in a male voice seemingly frees Lee to write more explicitly about desire and to express her own homoerotic desire in an unobjectionable manner.

Lee's final story in *Vanitas: Polite Stories,* "The Legend of Madame Krasinska," is similar to those in *Hauntings* in its depiction of the merging of the identities of a character from the past with one from the present, but the story seemingly has fewer erotic implications. It portrays an empathetic identification of one woman with another, as in "Oke of Okehurst," except that in this story the two women are contemporaries. This story depicts a same-sex merging of two women's identities, possibly as a coding of lesbian desire. A society woman takes on the identity of poor Sora Lena and, in so doing, takes on Sora Lena's role as social outcast, a mad streetwalker. "The Legend of Madame Krasinska," the story of the convent sister Mother Antoinette Marie, was told by the painter Cecchino Bandini to his friend, who becomes the story's narrator. Madame Krasinska, a society woman in Florence, obtains from Bandini the portrait of a well-known madwoman, Sora Lena, who is often seen wandering the city's streets. After Sora Lena dies by hanging herself, Madame Krasinska gradually assumes Sora Lena's identity, walking alone at night and dressing shabbily, as Sora Lena had done. Finally, Madame Krasinska is no longer herself, completely becoming the woman with whom she so identifies. Eventually Madame Krasinska tries to hang herself in the very room in which Sora Lena had died, but when she is cut down and rescued, she joins a convent, the Little Sisters of the Poor.

Lee is credited with inventing the English term "empathy," a quality that she demonstrates in her stories in this volume as well as in her other writings. All these stories demonstrate Lee's compelling ability to get into the mind and feelings of someone quite unlike herself and even of a different era. Peter Gunn rightly remarks on Lee's ability to give her historical novels and stories great authenticity, the "extraordinary ability of hers to 'feel herself into' (*empathetically*) a remote historical period, with an intensity of realization of the sentiments and passions of those then living. . . . " (Gunn, 225).

Two of Vernon Lee's stories in *Vanitas,* "Lady Tal" and "A Worldly Woman," are quite different in style and subject matter from those previously discussed. They are satiric portraits of men from whose point of view the stories are told. These men gradually reveal their own narcissism through their inner musings, particularly those about women with whom they are associated. In "Lady Tal" the man is a novelist, Jervase Marion, who is clearly modeled on Henry James. "A Worldly Woman" is told from the perspective of Leonard Greenleaf, a potter. In both stories the young women who have turned to these more mature and better-known men for professional advice as artists are viewed by the men as silly creatures with inferior minds. Nevertheless they captivate the men's interest through their intelligence and talent, showing the fallacy of men's belief in their artistic superiority, which supposedly justifies their domination of the arts.

"A Worldly Woman" and "Lady Tal" may have been Lee's revenge on Henry James for his criticism of her novel *Miss Brown.* That Lee was quite capable of caustic remarks is revealed in both her recorded conversations and her letters. *Miss Brown,* published in 1884, used fiction to launch a satiric attack on the aesthetic movement. Lee's dedication of that novel to Henry James was an embarrassment to him, since he found fault with the book artistically. Because of the dedication, James was reluctant to reveal the extent of his criticisms to Lee, but he finally did write out many of his objections in a letter to her.[4]

Lee uses James as the model for the male protagonists in her two satiric stories. Henry James was an easy target of satire, since his nuanced studies of women's minds and behavior indicate that he was arrogantly confident of his ability to understand women and interpret their actions. Both Leonard Greenleaf and Jervase Marion are represented as repressed men, coldly remote and haughty, who distance themselves from others, particularly from women, whom they treat as their inferiors. Lee says of Marion:

> Indeed, if Jervase Marion, ever since his earliest manhood, had given way to a tendency to withdraw from all personal concerns, from all emotion or action, it was mainly because he conceived that this shrinkingness of nature (which foolish persons called egoism) was the necessary complement to his power of intellectual analysis.[5]

Similarly, "Greenleaf lived so much more in his thoughts than in his life that creatures very speedily got to represent nothing but problems to him" (*V*, 162). Marion behaves like James, even sharing his mannerisms and physical characteristics. He is comically described as a novelist whose "books turned mainly upon the little intrigues and struggles of the highly civilized portion of society, in which only the fittest have survived, by virtue of talon and beak" (*V*, 35). Lest the reader fail to see the connection between James and Marion, the story explicitly states that Marion is "a kind of Henry James" (*V*, 11).

Both Greenleaf and Marion have a negative opinion of women generally, considering them stupid and ill-educated. Greenleaf, who is trying to teach Miss Valentine Flodden about ancient pottery, berates her for her lack of education. "He really could not realise the extraordinary emptiness in this young woman's mind" (*V*, 148–149). On another occasion Greenleaf believes he is desecrating the holy world of art by speaking about it to a woman: "What business had he to talk of such things to such a woman. To let the holy of holies become, most likely, a subject of mere idle curiosity and idle talk?" (*V*, 154). Since the story is told from Greenleaf's point of view, the reader contrasts Greenleaf's thoughts on Miss Flodden with her actions, which reveal her to be an intelligent and perceptive woman who is trying to educate herself because she lacks the formal education he was privileged to have.

Jervase Marion is similarly impatient with what he perceives as women's stupidity. While helping Lady Tal with her novel, he finds constant fault with it. He first plans to criticize it for its poor writing, complaining that "her grammar and spelling were nowhere" (*V*, 41). Then he decides the book is completely derivative, an imitation of others Lady Tal had read, when in fact it is clearly based on her own experiences. Like Greenleaf, Marion despises women, disparages their talent, and wants to distance himself from them. After spending time shopping with Lady Tal, Marion thinks, "What an odious, odious creature a woman is" (*V*, 62).

Through the character of Marion, Lee attacks male writers such as James for their parasitism. Marion takes only an abstract artistic interest in people in order to incorporate them into his fiction, as he is planning to do with Lady Tal in his next novel. "He was fully convinced that to study other folks and embody his studies in the most lucid form was the one mission of his life" (*V*, 53). Marion is a man with no heart, or so he reveals himself to be. He "did not give his heart, perhaps because he had none to give, to anybody" (*V*, 56). His visit to a hospital with Lady Tal makes him realize how divorced his writing is from life: "All this was not at all what he had imagined when he had occasionally written about young ladies consoling the sick" (*V*, 67). He repeatedly states that Lady Tal has no soul, and he thus finds her odious, but ironically he reveals himself to be the one with no soul or sympathetic feelings for others. Lee's portrait of James as a cold, heartless man who imagines he is a great novelist because he is a "dispassionate spectator of the world's follies and miseries" (*V*, 53) is devastatingly comic.

Lady Tal is not so clearly modeled on Vernon Lee as Marion is on Henry James, but Lady Tal has many similarities to Lee. For example, both Vernon Lee and Lady Tal had an invalid half-brother for whom they cared. Violet, Lee's actual name, is the name of the heroine of Lady Tal's novel *Christina,* which is really about Lady Tal herself. Just as Lee had dedicated *Miss Brown* to James, Lady Tal tells Marion she will dedicate her novel to him: "So I shall finish Christina, and print her, and publish her, and dedicate her to you" (*V*, 108). Marion's response is to smile politely and quickly run away from Lady Tal.

Lee also takes the criticism Marion gives of Lady Tal's novel from the criticism James had given of Lee's novel. In his letter to Lee about Miss Brown, James criticizes her creation of characters: " 'You have appealed too much to . . . (the intelligence, the moral sense and experience of the reader)' " (quoted in Gunn, 105). In "Lady Tal," Marion complains to Lady Tal that "your characters don't sufficiently explain themselves; you write as if your reader had witnessed the whole thing and merely required reminding" (*V*, 47).

Given Lee and James's rather strained relationship and their homo-erotic interests, the conclusion of the story is humorous: Lady Tal indirectly proposes to Marion, finally revealing her real power over him. He needs her to help him write his next novel. She declares that they can write a novel together because she can provide the novel's ending more satisfactorily than he can. She will have it end in marriage. Marion admits that in his novel the artist, who is modeled on himself, had acted as a fool. He recognizes his own deficiencies in understanding people's behavior, particularly women's. But we do not learn how he responds to Lady Tal's offer to collaborate on another novel or to her oblique marriage proposal.

Lee's satiric portrait of Leonard Greenleaf in "A Worldly Woman" represents an attack on asceticism. Greenleaf shares some of James's characteristics such as his remoteness and failure to understand women. Despite his condescending treatment of Valentine Flodden, Greenleaf is attracted to her. But he never reveals this to her and suddenly breaks off all contact with her. He has been reading James's *Princess Casamassima* and fears Val may be like the princess, "a horrible woman" (*V*, 191). He opts for a single life of work and solitude, rejecting Valentine. He believes his earlier experience of having his marriage proposal rejected turned out for the best: "His nature was too thin to allow of his giving himself both to a wife and family, and to the duties and studies which claimed him; he would have starved the affections of the first while neglecting the second. His life must always be a solitary one with his work" (*V*, 187).

The point of view of these two stories is that of men who dislike women, and yet work with them in an artistic collaboration. These women are revealed to be interesting and vital figures despite the men's harsh views of them. Lee's narrative method allows the men to expose themselves, with their own prejudices and limitations as artists, while at the same time the reader gains an accurate understanding and appreciation of the women these men so despise.

Lee's title *Vanitas: Polite Stories* is deeply ironic, since the stories are not polite but indiscreetly revelatory. They are polite only in the sense that they portray a seemingly genteel world, which masks its aggressions and anger. They certainly portray vanity, such as is revealed in Marion's arrogance about his knowledge of women. Needless to say, James was not amused by Lee's depiction of him in her stories, and his reaction to them was predictable. James wrote to his brother William James, warning him that Lee was dangerous and that her "books of fiction are a tissue of personalities of this hideous roman-à-clef kind" (quoted in Gunn, 138). The publication of these stories created a permanent rift in the relationship between Lee and James.

Lee's stories, with their gender "slippage" and homoerotic overtones, reveal an indebtedness to decadent writers. They also demonstrate Lee's understanding of the complexities of sexual desire. In her creation of strong women characters who attract men either through their enticing sexuality or by their intelligence, Lee expands the boundaries of the literary representation of women in the 1890s. Her unusual women do not know that they should be contained by a woman's sphere; rather, they function either as intelligent and creative women who exasperate traditional men or as haunting creatures capable of inspiring great passion and artistic power.

Chapter Seven

Fiction Written by Women for the *Yellow Book*

During the 1890s a number of literary periodicals began publication—notably the *Albemarle,* the *Savoy,* and the *Yellow Book.* In only one of these journals did women play any significant role, as either writers or editors: the *Yellow Book;* over one-third of its contributors were women. Although none of these periodicals was very long-lived, all were important in introducing new writers to the public and, with their inclusion of fiction and art, set a high literary tone for periodicals during the decade. The *Savoy,* which published eight issues, from January 1896 to December 1896, and was edited by Arthur Symons, contained fiction but never published any stories by women writers. The *Albemarle,* which ran from January to September 1892, contained little fiction but did carry stories by two women, F. Mabel Robinson and Alice Fleming, the sister of Rudyard Kipling. Even though women were scarcely represented as writers in the *Albemarle,* the journal was sympathetic in its treatment of women's issues and was important for advocating the cause of women. But the *Yellow Book* was the most important of the literary journals of the decade for women writers. It introduced many new women writers to an audience of elite and discriminating readers, which these writers would not otherwise have had.

The *Yellow Book* was published by Elkin Mathews and John Lane, who were also responsible for discovering and publishing in their Keynotes series relatively unknown writers—many of them women, such as George Egerton and Ella D'Arcy. With Henry Harland as its literary editor and Aubrey Beardsley as its art editor, the *Yellow Book,* devoted to literature and art, published 13 issues from April 1894 to April 1897. When the trial of Oscar Wilde and its accompanying notoriety became too closely associated with the periodical through Beardsley, Wilde's illustrator for *Salome,* Beardsley was removed as art editor after the first four volumes. Although Wilde had never been connected with the *Yellow Book* or contributed to it, Mrs. Humphrey Ward, believing in such a connection, agitated for the removal of Beardsley to save England from what she believed was moral peril.

Because of Beardsley's artwork for *Yellow Book,* many thought that the journal was primarily a vehicle of expression for decadent writers; this is an erroneous view that persists to this day. Nevertheless Beardsley was important to the journal for the many caricatured versions of the New Woman that he created in his drawings. His women possess many of the frightening qualities attributed to the New Women by their most out-spoken critics. Some of the women in Beardsley's drawings look as if they have more knowledge of the world than is proper; others are impos-ing figures of towering physical proportions. Extreme versions of the New Woman, they threaten to dominate men and corrupt other women with their sexual knowledge.

Such distorted images of women as Beardsley created are not really characteristic of those portrayed in stories written by women for the *Yellow Book.* Their fiction does depict women who dominate men, but generally the fictional women are more conventionally unpleasant than those drawn by Beardsley. Nevertheless, many of the stories by women in the *Yellow Book* reveal both societal anxiety about women, especially those who lack traditional feminine attributes and are too independent, and fears about women's sexuality that were shared by many people dur-ing the 1890s.

Some of the male contributors to the *Yellow Book* were already well-known literary figures, such as Henry James, George Moore, and George Gissing; but with the exception of George Egerton, the female contributors were not well known for their fiction when they first appeared in the journal. Later some of them published novels or collec-tions of short stories and established a greater reputation. For example, Netta Syrett and Evelyn Sharp both wrote novels that were included in Lane's Keynotes series, while Ada Leverson and Victoria Cross subse-quently wrote several novels. Because of its many and diverse contribu-tors, from Henry James to Max Beerbohm, as well as its commitment to high literary quality, the fiction writing of the *Yellow Book* has variety in its style and subject matter. However, the stories by both male and female writers belonged overwhelmingly to the realistic and naturalistic movement of the time, and the dominant tone of many of them was pessimistic.

The stories written by women writers for the *Yellow Book* do not advance any feminist cause but are characteristic of 1890s fiction generally. They include witty satires in the manner of Oscar Wilde, psychological thrillers, realistic tales of women's lives, and grim naturalistic stories of the fall of various women from respectability. What is missing is fiction typical of that created by the New Woman writers with their more liberated and outspoken heroines. The stories by the women writers in the *Yellow Book* did not overtly advocate any social changes that would benefit women, as did many of the more didactic novels of the period. In fact, women's stories in the *Yellow Book* rarely directly challenged the prevailing gender ideology of earlier fiction of the century. Far from representing advanced ideas of liberated sexuality, most of the short stories were conventional and in some cases reactionary in their depiction of gender roles. Even Egerton's two stories in the *Yellow Book,* "A Lost Masterpiece" in Volume I and "The Captain's Book" in Volume VI, are quite unlike her stories in *Keynotes* and *Discords.* The first story, "A Lost Masterpiece," uses the impressionistic style and stream-of-consciousness technique of many of her other stories, but neither story in the journal depicts the interesting women characters, with their rich fantasy lives and uninhibited sexuality, that were so captivating to the female readers of Egerton's *Keynotes.*

Many of the stories in the journal by both men and women construct many different versions of women's identity, showing a great fascination with women, particularly with their sexuality. This interest in woman's nature and her sexuality reflected the interest of much of the fiction of the decade, particularly the novels by New Woman writers but also the fiction of male writers such as Thomas Hardy and George Meredith. But few of the stories by women in the *Yellow Book* challenge traditional views of women and of female psychology in the radical ways that many novels by women did. Many of the stories represent women's sexuality as threatening in that it is a disruptive and destabilizing force destructive of men and family life.

The *Yellow Book,* despite its reputation for being new and avant-garde, contained fiction—particularly by women—that reflected a more traditional gender ideology than was found in many women's novels of the decade, such as those included in Lane's Keynotes series. But in their depiction of the distorted and unpleasant characters of women, the stories by women writers certainly issue as powerful an indictment of social conditions for women as that given by the much more outspoken New Women writers.

Ella D'Arcy (1851–1937?) was the most important woman associated with the *Yellow Book.* After Henry Harland, the literary editor, she was the most prolific contributor to the journal. Eleven of her stories were included, one in almost every issue. She also served unofficially as Harland's assistant and was most likely responsible for the inclusion in the journal of stories by so many women writers. In her own stories in the *Yellow Book,* many of which were later collected in *Monochromes* (1895) and *Modern Instances* (1898), D'Arcy deals frankly and realistically with the woman and the marriage question. By portraying women in their relationships with men as the victimizers as often as they are the victims, she shows how destructive women can be without any intellectual or creative outlets for their energies.

In D'Arcy's first story in Volume I of the *Yellow Book,* "Irremediable," a man is lured into marriage by a foolish young woman he meets on his vacation. He first notices "that she was young and that she was not what is called 'a lady'—of which he was glad."[1] Initially he finds charm in "talking nonsense with a girl who was natural, simple-minded" (*YB* I, 91), but after marriage he discovers only boring stupidity. His life is destroyed by her manipulations and pettiness. Not only is she decidedly ignorant; she is also unable to maintain any semblence of order or cleanliness in the house. The man's intense anguish at the end of the story at the prospect of the many years ahead with a woman so unlike himself, with whom he cannot share any intellectual life, provides a contrast to many of the women's novels of the decade, which depicted women trapped in unhappy marriages with boorish and insensitive men. In this story, the man is represented as superior in his education and social standing to his wife, who is seemingly to blame for the many ills of their marriage. She entraps him by acting as if she were helpless and then entices him with her sexual charm.

In D'Arcy's stories, women behave as badly as men, and often worse; their powerless position in society drives them to commit vindictive and destructive acts. D'Arcy's story "A Marriage," which appeared in Volume XI of the *Yellow Book,* is similar to "Irremediable" in that it also portrays a man who becomes entangled in an unpleasant situation when he marries a woman who has already borne his child. She is from a lower social background than he and over the years becomes shrewish, petty, and demanding. Like the heroine of "Irremediable," this woman marries a man who has the social and intellectual advantages of his class, and she then destroys his life through her narrow, small-minded concerns. In D'Arcy's story "A Marriage," the man's destruction is also physical, leading to death, a condition which in these stories becomes a metaphor for the loss of the man's sexuality and power.

The women in these stories seem to be designing villains in their destruction of worthy men. However, the real blame for such unhappy relationships lies with the social conditions that produced such ignorant women. Although the stories appear to blame women unnecessarily for their narrow lives and frivolous concerns, they can more accurately be read as an indictment of a system that deprives women of the education necessary for the intellectual development that would enable them to form equal alliances with educated men. D'Arcy's female characters do not articulate such advanced ideas; neither do her men recognize that their disastrous personal relations are the consequence of social injustice. But implicitly, D'Arcy's stories provide evidence that conditions for women need to change if their lives—and men's also—are to improve. As if in confirmation of the ideas of other writers such as Mona Caird and Sarah Grand about social issues relating to women, D'Arcy realistically portrays women's lives as they have become—distorted and constricted by their narrow experiences. Women are denied educational and economic opportunities and are trained to be parasites on men rather than intelligent individuals capable of leading independent lives.

D'Arcy shows the price women pay for respectability by portraying her more socially acceptable female characters as dull, lifeless creatures who suppress their own sexuality, pursue marriage as a social and economic necessity, and lead narrow, conventional lives. One must look to women of the lower classes to find passion and life, but this vitality comes at a price. "At Twickenham" articulates some of D'Arcy's criticism of contemporary women through the character of Dr. Matheson, who breaks off his engagement to a perfectly nice woman because she is too much like most English girls: "too good, too normal, too well-regulated" (*YB* XII, 331). He yearns for someone with soul and feeling and warmth who is "capable of a very passionate affection" (*YB* XII, 331).

Although D'Arcy's stories contain a great variety of women, few of them are admirable. Her women characters are foolish and irrational, as is the case of those in "White Magic," and they are scheming and greedy, as are those in "Poor Cousin Louis." The pharmacist in "White Magic" tells the story of a young girl who comes to him for dragon's blood to make a love potion in order to recapture her estranged lover. The pharmacist describes the girl as irrational and superstitious. Women are the same everywhere, he says; "one need never hope to prevail through wisdom with a woman" (*YB* III, 67). Although the story never calls such sentiments into question or deconstructs them in any way, the love that the young couple finds at the end through the supposed love potion contradicts the glib generalities of the pharmacist. Even if the love is realized through an irrational belief in dragon's blood, it is nonetheless real. "Poor Cousin Louis" (*YB* II) depicts greedy women stealing from a dying man, but the men in the story behave no better. In fact, the doctor tending the patient, Cousin Louis, more or less condones letting the man die so that he and the servants can all benefit.

A common theme of D'Arcy's stories and many other stories written by women for the *Yellow Book,* such as Netta Syrett's "Far Above Rubies" and "Thy Heart's Desire," is that of female entrapment and male emasculation. Women's destructive behavior is part of a larger issue that so many of the stories deal with in a covert manner: women's sexuality out of control. Women use their sexuality to entice men, who then suffer in the relationship. That so many stories use such a plot reveals the fear felt by both men and women at the thought of any change in the traditional role of man as the dominant pursuer of a submissive female. Not only does the woman's self-assertiveness make her a figure to be condemned by society; it also leads to the destruction of the man's virility and occasionally even his life.

Many of these stories, such as "Irremediable" and "A Marriage," depict relationships between men and women from different social classes, the woman invariably being the lower-class individual. It is easier to attribute shameless use of sexuality to lower-class women because such women supposedly lack the social inhibitions of those above them. The reason that the men are attracted to these women is seldom questioned by D'Arcy or the other women writers. Many of the stories in the *Yellow Book* reveal both the traps of sexuality set by women and the dangers inherent in marrying outside one's class. Women in these stories advance themselves socially through marriage, but the same energy that activated them to pursue a man above them eventually enervates the man and destroys his masculinity. At the conclusion of D'Arcy's "Irremediable," the husband, unable to stand up to his wife's tirades, finds that his only passion is inspired by his present hatred of the wife who so charmed him before their marriage.

Even though many of her stories show unhappy relationships between men and women, D'Arcy employs a generous variety of plots and tells her stories from the point of view of both men and women. Several of her stories are mysterious thrillers with unexpected endings. Vernon Lee also wrote some stories, although not for the *Yellow Book,* that have the same psychological complexity, mysterious events, and often surprising conclusions as those by D'Arcy. "The Villa Lucienne" (*YB* X) contains a haunted house that visitors suspect was the site of a murder. In "The Web of Maya" (*YB* VII) a man confesses to a murder that he wanted to commit and actually believes he did commit. Feeling guilty, he then is told by the man to whom he confesses that the supposed victim is still alive. Instead of being relieved, he again wishes the man dead and presumably will try again to kill him. "Sir Julian Garve" (*YB* XIII) has an unexpected and shocking murder at its conclusion. In "The Pleasure-Pilgrim" (*YB* V) D'Arcy combines a love interest with a sudden death by gunshot. Whether the frustrated lover means to kill herself or dies by accident is unclear both to the reader and to the man with whom she is in love. D'Arcy's more mysterious stories show the complexity of the unconscious, with its ability to create alternative realities.

Netta Syrett, the niece of Grant Allen, provides a further example of a predatory and destructive woman in "Far Above Rubies" (*YB* XII). In this story the aggressive woman, Mrs. Gilman, is again from the lower classes and has married into wealth. Mrs. Gilman, bored with her husband, flirts with the young doctor who visits their house professionally. She is openly seductive, but when he kisses her, she tells her husband and destroys the doctor's practice. Financially ruined, the doctor is forced to leave town. Mrs. Gilman's vindictive nature and blatant sexuality are represented as relating to her lower-class origins. The title, "Far Above Rubies," is an ironic reference to the biblical description of a virtuous woman who is not represented in the story. In another of Syrett's stories in the *Yellow Book,* "Thy Heart's Desire" (*YB* II), Kathleen Drayton marries a man she does not love, then falls in love with another man, Broomhurst, when he visits her and her husband in a remote area of India. When her husband dies—seemingly by suicide after contemplating his wife's possible infidelity—and she returns to England, Broomhurst visits her, asking her to marry him. She says she no longer loves him and now will not marry without love.

In her depiction of the powers of Mrs. Gilman and Kathleen Drayton, Syrett shows the strength of female sexuality. These women seduce and abandon men, causing destruction and death—a reversal of the usual plot of seduced and abandoned women. But reversing these roles hardly means that the women are liberated in the context of these stories. They are instead portrayed as heartless beings whose desire to express their own feelings openly is represented as reprehensible and destabilizing.

Such thinking on women's behavior is continued in Menie Muriel Dowie's "An Idyll in Millinery." Lord Liphook falls in love with a young French girl in a millinery shop, but, in what is presented as a fortunate circumstance for him, just as he is planning to ask her to marry him, she is sent back to France to marry someone else. While he is resolving to pursue her to Paris, someone calls his name: "His world had claimed him" (*YB* X, 53), meaning he returns to his class's thinking as to who is suitable for marriage and in so doing luckily escapes the clutches of the French girl. For men to marry women of a class below them is dangerous, and not just for economic reasons. The men are attracted to the more liberated sexuality of lower-class women, but they must resist it because it will be the means of destroying them, literally or psychically, after marriage.

In some *Yellow Book* stories, through the reversal of male forms, women sometimes take on the profligacy of the Victorian male villain by stepping outside their prescribed gender roles. These women who pursue their own sexual pleasure are destructive not only of the men who love them but of their children as well. In Lena Milman's "Marcel: An Hotel-Child" (*YB* XII), an American boy is moved about Europe, from hotel to hotel, by a divorced mother who cares more about her Italian lover than her own son. She even deserts her son when he is ill in order to join her lover elsewhere. In his loneliness the son turns to the Roman Catholic church for solace and, on his deathbed, interchanges in his imagination the Madonna figure with that of his mother. The grim conclusion of so many of these stories can be attributed to conventional gender roles gone awry.

The women in the stories who use their sexuality to advance their social position or to ensnare an unsuspecting man are shown to be odious figures who have eschewed their traditional role in society, but poor women, who are the more traditional figures of Victorian fiction, fare even worse. These women get pregnant and are then abandoned. "Martha," by Mrs. Murray Hickson (Mabel Kitcat), chronicles the fate of a poor country girl, Martha, who is hired at a boarding house and soon "got herself into trouble" (*YB* VII, 278). Turned out with nowhere to go, she simply disappears into a world which "shows little of mercy, and even less of sympathy and comprehension" (*YB* VII, 279). Her plight is the more tragic and ironic in that it is the women in the boarding house who show no sympathy for her poverty, abuse her while she is in service, and then force her out without a thought when she becomes pregnant. Even the woman who narrates the story, after showing some initial interest in Martha, neglects her.

Charlotte Mew's only story in the *Yellow Book*, "Passed" (*YB* II), also shows the destructive effects of poverty on the lives of women, forcing them to turn to prostitution to escape starvation. This naturalistic story, set in the slums of London, has a grim tone, reflecting Mew's personal experience with a life of poverty and despair. Mew herself committed suicide in 1928. The narrator of this story leaves her home one evening to wander the city's streets. On this journey, which seems like a descent into hell, she finds continual evidence of the desperation of women's lives. The cries of women and screams of children meet her ears, as does the sight of lonely girls and women. Then, in a window, she sees a picture of a girl at prayer, whose eyes are turned to heaven but whose breasts are bare. This image, borrowed from paintings of Mary Magdalene as a penitent prostitute, combines allusions to sensuality and purity. The narrator turns from the picture "sickly away" (*YB* II, 124). After that she is brought to the home of two women, one of whom is lying dead with a look of disillusion on her face, the implication being that she had been abandoned by a man. But the narrator herself then abandons the other woman, who is alone and starving and who pleads with her to stay. Months later, when she sees that woman on the street dressed as a prostitute and on the arm of a man, she thinks, "I knew my part then in the despoiled body" (*YB* II, 141).

"Passed" is filled with pictures of women's lives gone awry—of women destroyed by men and abandoned by other women. For poor women to seek purity or respectability is a foolish goal if they are to survive. The portrait of the woman's heavenward gaze and bared breasts accurately suggests the alternatives for women: a desire for purity but an acknowledgement of what sells. Mew's story, as well as Hickson's "Martha," implicitly calls for sympathy for the plight of poor women whose wretched lives end in prostitution and suicide. But the women who narrate the stories, while sympathetically depicting women's lives, themselves fail to provide any real help. Both stories are an indictment of women's failure to show solidarity with other women, particularly those outside their social class, or to act on their behalf.

The stories also show that the life of the single woman who acts conventionally, according to social expectations, is not a happy one either. A happy single woman is a rare creature in 1890s fiction. In Leila Macdonald's "Jeanne-Marie," the woman of the title is an unmarried sister who is displaced from her home when her brother marries. Her loneliness increases when her sister-in-law blames her for her nephew's illness and she no longer sees him. Although she has lingering pain from a heart attack, her real heart pains result from the anger she feels at being accursed—never having had a husband or children. Jeanne-Marie leads a life of desperate loneliness; her only consolation comes at death, when the priest prays over her, saying, "Blessed be the virgins above all women" (*YB* III, 240), and a measure of joy is found through projected happiness in the afterlife.

The young woman in Ada Radford's "Lot 99" (*YB* XI) studies and tries to educate herself, wanting to be a teacher, since she believes she will never marry; but self-education does not give her any better prospect for happiness. She capitulates to her brother's wish for her to stay at home. The story ends with the same melancholy tone as Macdonald's.

Another of Ada Radford's stories, "Lucy Wren," also reflects the desperate loneliness of the single woman. Lucy Wren is a teacher of girls, but she believes that educating girls cannot bring them happiness unless the education gives them other choices in life than marriage. She falls in love with a married man, but when she hears the man's wife and her friends gossiping about a governess who flirted with someone's husband—"And tale after tale of the audacity of their sex went the round of the party" (*YB* XIII, 283)—she realizes what her position would be if she responded to that love.

Although many of the stories vilify women who act on their feelings, women who suppress their emotions and fail to act do not achieve happy lives either. A woman in Marion Hepworth Dixon's "A Thief in the Night" (*YB* IV) creeps during the night to the room of her husband's dead brother, the man she had really loved, to find some memory of him. She takes his dressing gown and goes back to her room, hugging it.

None of these stories envisions a satisfactory life for a woman outside life with a man. A woman's only value comes from her alliance with a man; and the more important he is, the more highly she is esteemed. An old servant of a young painter in Paris, in Ella Hepworth Dixon's "The Sweet o' the Year" (*YB* IX), gains new status in the painter's eyes when she brings out old love letters written to her by a famous painter long ago. Apparently she was once beautiful and sexually desirable, and proof of that is an indication of her worth.

Unlike many of the novels of the decade, these stories contain no communities of supportive women but rather women eager to support the social restrictions from which they also suffer. Rather than finding natural allies in other women in an effort to change the system, women are driven by economic necessity to form alliances with those who oppress them. Women are pitted against one another in a marriage market in which its many losers face a poverty-stricken existence. The social and economic systems have failed to accommodate the unmarried woman.

The few stories in the *Yellow Book* which are lighthearted and comic in tone are almost fanciful, as if they were fairy tales, not to be construed as serious possibilities. Evelyn Sharp writes several such stories. "The Restless River" (*YB* XII) is the tale of a prince who rejects ruling, defies the queen, and marries the woman he loves, a woodcutter's daughter, who emerges from a river in which she was drowned as a child. The prince cares nothing for rank but follows his heart. His godfather, at his christening, had given him the gift of being a true lover, apparently a rare quality for a man, especially a prince. In "The Other Anna" (*YB* XIII), a woman of some social standing poses as an artist's model, a job usually relegated to lower-class women. She does this as a joke when the artist initially mistakes her for a model. She and the artist are attracted to each other, but his belief that she is beneath him socially allows them to have a more open relationship than is conducive to falling in love. His realization finally that she is of his class then makes possible a happy ending. Both of these comic stories by Sharp use the same motif as many of the more tragic ones—men's attraction to women who are supposedly their social inferiors.

The one story by Vernon Lee (Violet Paget) in the *Yellow Book,* "Prince Alberic and the Snake Lady" (*YB* X), is also about devoted love. It is fanciful, told like a child's tale, with a prince, a wicked king, and a beautiful woman who spends most of her time as a snake. The snake lady first becomes important to Prince Alberic when as a boy he becomes passionately attached to her image as represented on a tapestry of Alberic the Blond, the prince's ancestor, and the snake woman Oriana. When the tapestry is removed from his room, it is replaced with one depicting Susanna and the elders, which Alberic destroys in a rage. For this act he is banished from the castle. In his new home, set in a garden of Eden type of world with plants and animals, a snake visits him. This is not the evil snake of Eden but a beautiful, loving woman, the snake woman depicted on the tapestry. Alberic learns that if a man of his family is faithful to her for 10 years, the snake will become a woman permanently. Alberic keeps the snake in his room, which each day briefly becomes a woman, until the evil king kills it and Alberic dies of grief.

Like the prince in Sharp's story "The Restless River," Alberic is a devoted lover who defies a royal demand that he must marry someone of rank. Alberic loves the snake woman of the tapestry and then the snake woman herself; clearly he rejects the licentious view of love represented in the tapestry of Susanna and the elders in favor of a commitment to faithful love and eternal devotion. Such perfect love and such faithful men as the princes in Sharp's and Lee's stories are not found in real life. These fantastic stories are set in an unreal realm. Even within the stories love is experienced apart from society, in a house in the woods, in an Edenesque garden, or in a room alone with a tapestry or snake. Even in a fairy-tale world perfect love which defies parental and societal disapproval can be realized only in a place removed from society.

The one woman writer who provides satiric stories for the *Yellow Book,* with comic and irreverant characters who use the flippant dialogue of characters out of Oscar Wilde, is Ada Leverson, who was a close friend of Wilde's and maintained her loyalty to him before, during, and after his imprisonment. Her stories catch some of Wilde's humor. They reflect no desire for fidelity or domesticity and are replete with lines that could have been taken from one of Wilde's plays; for example, "Every one admits he's fascinating; he is very popular and very much disliked" (*YB* V, 255).

In Leverson's "Suggestion" (*YB* V), Cecil Carington, a rather smug young man, arranges love affairs, including that of his father, who marries Laura, a young friend of Cecil's sister Marjorie. The mocking tone of the story—with its confusion of lovers and with young men who behave like dandies, arranging affairs and exhibiting no concern for fidelity—stands in complete contrast to the rest of the stories by women in the *Yellow Book,* which depict the seriousness of the relationship between the sexes. Gone is the grim realism; it is replaced by a satiric treatment of Wilde's amoral world, which mocks bourgeois values and the marriage game. But this is not a world in which women have a role beyond being playthings for men's comic romantic escapades. Leverson's stories implicitly comment on the single man's comic and romantic adventures, which contrast so tellingly with the single woman's grim experiences portrayed in the fiction of the decade. Her other story, "The Quest for Sorrow" (*YB* VIII), relates a search by the same smug Cecil Carington for some tragedy in his life, which he believes can be gained by his experiencing unrequited love. His only problem is that every woman he pretends to like loves him, and he must finally escape to the beaches of France with the realization that unhappiness will forever be denied him.

Both of Leverson's comedies are told by the young man Cecil Carington, a rather obnoxious and conceited twit, whose self-absorption and dandified manner are certainly taken from Oscar Wilde and other decadents. The stories make lighthearted fun of relationships between the sexes, revealing the desire for love to be part of the usual quest of any

young man for sex and pleasure, not the serious desire for security that
so many stories present it to be. But we get a male point of view in
Leverson's stories, and a rich male's point of view at that. The women's
feelings in both stories are of no account. It is hard to imagine a woman's
voice telling a tale about her longing for unrequited love. Leverson
directs her satire toward the egotistical male narrator who cares nothing
for women except as they provide comic adventure in his life. She also is
satirizing Wilde and other vain dandies of the 1890s.

The *Yellow Book* contains an abundance of stories written by women
but narrated from a male point of view. That fact may partially account
for the rather dismal depiction of women's lives and the strong disapproval given to so many of the women's actions. The male narrator
speaks as the voice of society in its disapproval of the actions of women,
failing to understand the conditions of their lives. By using male narrators, women are demonstrating their lack of voice or language to define
their own experiences. Thus the ironic use of the male narrator providing
a male commentary on women's lives exemplifies the very powerlessness
of women that the stories themselves illustrate.

"Theodora: A Fragment" by Victoria Cross (Vivian Cory) is unlike
most stories by women written for the *Yellow Book* in its decidedly decadent presentation of sexual ambivalence. In the male narrator's discussion of his attraction to Theodora, he emphasizes her androgynous
appearance as important to his desire for her. He says that Theodora
"looked so like a young fellow of nineteen" (*YB* IV, 167). She has "a dash
of virility, a hint at dissipation, a suggestion of a certain decorous loose-
ness of morals" (*YB* IV, 162). Theodora's magnificent shoulders and
small waist emphasize her androgynous appeal. The narrator admits that
his desire for her is not guided by natural instinct, because he then
would want a more womanly person with a more feminine physique.
While admiring her body, he downplays its feminine characteristics,
instead pointing out the slightness of her breasts, which give "little suggestion of the duties or powers of Nature, but with infinite seduction for
a lover" (*YB* IV, 175).

The narrator's attraction to androgynous lovers is often reinforced in
the story. His book of sketches made during his journey to the east contains portraits mostly of men but also of androgynous figures or figures
of uncertain gender. He has obviously had a series of lovers, seemingly of
both genders—or at least many desired lovers—before he meets
Theodora; he wonders at one point whether she is not his new object of
desire. The narrator is drawn by the sexual ambiguity he finds in

Theodora's physique and in her actions, which alternate from passivity to assertiveness. At his home she puts on the clothing of an eastern man, with jacket and fez, and the narrator is overcome with desire. But she had arrived at his home dressed as a man, in a velvet jacket and a small hat resembling a fez. The sketches indicated earlier that the narrator's attraction to an individual has a racial as well as a gender component. This interest in the supposedly exotic is in evidence when Theodora transforms herself from western to eastern by putting on eastern clothing. In so doing, she stimulates in him a desire that contains all the ambiguities of gender and race.

Theodora is the femme fatale of decadent art and fiction, the enticing woman who destroys her lover or leaves him unsatisfied. Her behavior, alternating from passion to passivity, demonstrates the fluidity of feminine desire. Throughout the story the narrator emphasizes the "strange mingling of extremes" in Theodora, from passion to passivity, from weakness to independent determination. She denounces Shiva, who he says is the Hindu god of self-denial but who is actually the god of destruction, and she warns about the penalties suffered for rejecting nature's laws; and the narrator reads her pronouncements as a sexual invitation to him. He desires to dominate her, since she has seduced him and left him unsatisfied. But when he is overcome with desire and madly kisses her, her lips are passive.

The story is called a "fragment" because we do not learn how this affair concludes. Cross rejects the traditional ending—marriage—and provides a far more open-ended and ambiguous conclusion. The characters desire the instability of a passionate relationship over the stability of marriage. The story is also a fragment because this tale of seduction has a decidedly one-sided telling. How responsive Theodora is to the narrator's passion is not made clear. Victoria Cross creates a story about a man supposedly seduced by a woman, but we cannot tell whether she is consciously seducing him or whether his overwrought senses, responding to her androgynous appearance and exotic attire, read more into her actions than is there. She is more a creation of the male imagination than a real woman. Like Vernon Lee in her decadent stories in *Hauntings,* Cross lets a man narrate this story of obsessive desire for a woman, and in so doing, she suggests that decadent writing belongs to men and can be appropriated by women writers only if they have a man tell the tale. Using a male voice, Cross creates a far more interesting demonstration of the complexities of sexual desire than is present in most of the stories by women in the *Yellow Book.*

The most unusual and interesting stories written by women for the *Yellow Book,* such as those by Ada Leverson and Victoria Cross, abandon the realism and naturalism characteristic of the majority of the stories. They adopt modes more typical of some of the male writers of the 1890s, particularly the decadents, employing their satiric tone and psychological complexity. But a great many of the women's stories of all types written for the journal are told from a male point of view or by a male narrator. The use of the masculine voice reinforces the reader's perception that the stories women wrote for the *Yellow Book* are more typical of those being written by mainstream male writers during the decade than they are of the novels being published by the New Woman writers. These stories by women about women also demonstrate, through their masculine telling of women's lives, the very powerlessness which distorts the personalities of these fictional women. What is lacking in so many of the stories, which the novels of the time exhibited, is women's resistance to their lot and a determination to change the conditions of their lives. Nevertheless they implicitly make the same plea for social change that the fiction by New Women overtly demanded.

Chapter Eight

Women Writers of the 1890s and Their Twentieth-Century Critics

By the end of the nineteenth century, interest in the women writers of the 1890s who had created such controversy with their fiction of revolt had abruptly declined, and most of their novels were already out of print. Although many of these women, including Grand, Caird, Egerton, and Cholmondeley, continued to publish fiction in the twentieth century, their work received little attention and few reviews. Grand's biographer Gillian Kersley says that by the time Grand died in 1943, half a century after "gaining notoriety as the author of *The Heavenly Twins,* her obituarists on both sides of the Atlantic could scarcely remember her" (Kersley, 334).

The canon for the decade, the fiction through which the period was studied and remembered, was almost exclusively by male writers such as Thomas Hardy, George Gissing, George Moore, and George Meredith. Even the New Woman heroine was examined as she was portrayed by male writers. Early studies of the artistic and literary life of the decade, such as Holbrook Jackson's *The Eighteen Nineties: A Review of Art and Ideas at the Close of the Nineteenth Century,* published in 1925, focused almost exclusively on male writers. Jackson only briefly mentions some of the women fiction writers, despite the immense popularity of their novels during the 1890s. Not until the 1970s did critics, influenced by feminist criticism and the new historicism, begin a serious examination of women's fiction of the 1890s. However, many of these critics devalued the work of these women writers on the same grounds as did the critics of the 1890s: its stylistic deficiencies and its overt polemics.

A. R. Cunningham's essay, "The 'New Woman Fiction' of the 1890's" (1973), provides one of the first critical assessments in this century of some of these novelists. Cunningham distinguishes two main types of New Woman novelists: those of the purity school, such as Sarah Grand and Iota, who dealt with the marriage question with a new frankness; and those depicting more nervous and sensitive heroines. According to Cunningham, the latter group, which was more radical in its treatment of women's sexuality, included writers such as George Egerton, Emma Frances Brooke, Mona Caird, and Menie Muriel Dowie. Although the New Woman novels of the decade do not fit neatly into such exclusive categories, to which critics of the 1890s had first assigned them, Cunningham's analysis of these women's contributions to the New Woman fiction is important in that it recognizes the writers' emphasis on women's sexual nature, their treatment of such topics as venereal disease and prostitution, and their contributions to changing the image of women in fiction. Even though Cunningham does not believe that these writers "produced works of lasting merit," he states that "their contribution to both the feminist cause and the development of the English novel of the period should not be underestimated. The way was paved for a more realistic characterization of women in fiction to match their increasing social emancipation. . . . "[1]

In 1977, with the publication of *A Literature of Their Own: British Women Novelists from Brontë to Lessing,* Elaine Showalter brought to public attention many forgotten women writers, including some from this decade. Showalter discusses these writers in relationship to the development of women's fiction in the preceding century. The generation of writers before these she calls "feminine" novelists; the writers of the 1890s she labels as "feminists," saying that they "played a central role in the formulation and popularization of feminist ideology" (182). The feminists protested against the standards and values that the earlier generation of women writers, the feminine writers, had imitated and internalized (Showalter 1977, 13). Showalter says of these later writers:

> The feminists challenged many of the restrictions on women's self-expression, denounced the gospel of self-sacrifice, attacked patriarchal religion, and constructed a theoretical model of female oppression . . . Making their fiction the vehicle for a dramatization of wronged womanhood, they demanded changes in the social and political systems that would grant women male privileges and require chastity and fidelity from men. (Showalter 1977, 29)

Showalter's study is important for its recognition of the place these writers occupy in the development of women's fiction. Besides providing an analysis of some of the fiction of Sarah Grand and George Egerton, Showalter also introduces the names of other writers from the period, such as Menie Muriel Dowie and Mona Caird, whose fiction had been almost completely forgotten. Despite her recognition of these writers in 1977, which began an important reexamination of their fiction by other critics, Showalter, as did other critics, claimed that these women were responsible for their own literary demise. They did not fare well with posterity because they were engaged in a quarrel that "leads to rhetoric but not poetry" (Showalter 1977, 193). She devalues their writing, stating that "all the feminists had but one story to tell, and exhausted themselves in its narration" (Showalter 1977, 215).

Two other books from the late 1970s also examined the women writers of this period. Gail Cunningham's *The New Woman and the Victorian Novel* (1978), although largely devoted to a study of men who were considered to be New Woman writers, has an important chapter on the fiction of sex and the New Woman. In it, Cunningham accounts for the immense interest in many of the women writers of the 1890s during their time. Cunningham gives greater significance to these writers than previous critics, believing they had an important effect on literature:

> Firstly, by joining with such relish in the new movement to liberate fiction, and doing so on the wave of a popular debate about the liberation of women, they broke through the constricting bounds of conventional reticence and helped clear a path for better novelists to tread relatively unmolested. And secondly they provide a necessary context in which to judge the sudden emergence of feminist propaganda in the works of writers whose claims to attention on literary merit are securely established. (G. Cunningham, 79)

Patricia Stubbs's *Women and Fiction: Feminism and the Novel 1880–1920* (1979) is also largely devoted to male writers such as Thomas Hardy, George Moore, and George Meredith. Stubbs looks briefly at the short stories of Ella D'Arcy and George Egerton, contrasting their depictions of women: D'Arcy, the realist, exposes the selfishness and destructiveness of women while Egerton, an idealist and a romantic, portrays the potential within women and posits an ideal future for them. Stubbs dismisses what she calls the "transient feminist novels of the 'nineties," calling them "treatises first, novels second. Many were confused and sentimental, or bald statements of problems rather than attempts to come to grips with them."[2] Finding the feminist novelists of the 1890s deficient in literary talent, Stubbs declares that

> [they] just were not good enough *as* writers to turn their material into an important challenge to the literary tradition. This meant that at the very moment when literature was beginning to break free from the moral stranglehold of Victorian sexual ideology, the novel was dominated for the first time and quite accidentally by male writers. (Stubbs, 120)

Despite her rather bleak assessment of the literary talent of these writers, whose deficiencies she believed accounted for the fact that the novel of the decade was taken over by men "quite accidentally," Stubbs still provides interesting information on the backlash or counterattack against the sexual honesty of women's novels. She documents many of the attacks on feminism found in both the daily and the periodical presses and in subsequent novels such as those by George Gissing and Henry James. These attacks would certainly indicate that men's appropriation of the novel, particularly the New Woman novel, was not entirely as accidental as Stubbs herself believed.

David Rubinstein's *Before the Suffragettes: Women's Emancipation in the 1890s* (1986) puts the literary contributions of women, particularly the New Woman writers, in a wider context, discussing women's educational, economic, and political advances during the decade. The fiction of revolt was just one manifestation of the demands being made by women for emancipation, and it played an important role in women's struggle. Rubinstein says that "at no time in the history of English women's struggle for emancipation can fiction have played such an important part as in the 1890s" (Rubinstein, 24). Women challenged the conditions of their lives through their literature, thus advancing their social and political agenda. Rubinstein agrees with Showalter's idea that it was during this decade that the first "overtly feminist novels" were published (Rubinstein, 25). After recognizing women's contribution to fiction during this decade and fiction's contribution to women's emancipation, Rubinstein concludes his assessment of these writers as had many critics before him:

> The feminists of the 1890s contributed little of permanent value to the development of English fiction, but the courage and forcefulness with which they opened new aspects of the case for women's emancipation amply deserve the recognition which they have begun belatedly to receive." (Rubinstein, 33–34)

More recent critics, while not making any extravagant claims for the literary stature of these women writers, have examined the reasons for the historic opposition to them. Two studies published during the 1990s provide an explanation for the earlier and continued denegration of these women writers, particularly in terms of their literary ability and their place in literary history. Ann L. Ardis's *New Women, New Novels: Feminism and Early Modernism* (1990) examines reasons for the marginalization of the New Woman novels. By deviating from the dominant Victorian ideal of femininity, becoming inseparable from the politics of the time, and blurring the lines between popular and high art fiction, these novels threatened the critical establishment.

The aesthetic deficiency from which these novels were and are believed to have suffered, Ardis believes, resulted from their defiance of formalist assumptions about the unity of a work. She believes that the formalist aesthetic associated with high modernism devalued the New Woman novels, with their very political and controversial stances. Ardis's book also discusses the challenge of New Woman novels to traditional ideology. She sees the New Woman novels as the precursors of modernism in their challenging of narrative convention and their experimentation with new kinds of heroines.

Lyn Pykett's *The 'Improper' Feminine: The Women's Sensation Novel and the New Woman Writing* (1992) focuses on two literary developments in the nineteenth century in which women writers played an important part: the sensation novels of the 1860s and the New Woman fiction of the 1890s. Women's fiction in both periods was "improper" because it was perceived as invading a masculine world of rationality and impartiality with feminine feeling and intuition. Writers of both groups—the sensation and the New Woman writers—focused on women's lives to show the contradictions between the dominant ideology of the feminine and the actual lives of women. Both groups raised public anxieties and generated controversy.

Pykett believes the New Woman writers reproduced the contradictions that characterized late-Victorian ideas of the feminine. By challenging gender boundaries in paradoxical ways—behaving mannishly as well as hysterically with hyperfemininity—women moved out of the realm of the "proper" feminine, their regulated role which supposedly ensured national health. Because the gendered discourse of the nineteenth century fixed gender categories, the "improper" feminine was viewed as subversive. It signified chaos, impropriety, blatant sexuality, and immorality. By disrupting gender categories, these women, both the sensation novelists and the New Woman writers, became contradictory figures.

Recent critics, including Ardis and Pykett, in discussing the women writers of the 1890s, feel no necessity to place an abstract literary value on their fiction. Because the canon today is in flux, instead of deciding who the best writers of the decade are, critics can ask more interesting questions about the fiction of this time, such as: Against what social and literary conventions are these writers revolting? What was the nature of the backlash against them, and why was it stated in such apocalyptic

terms? Why did some male writers join the backlash in the representation of women in their fiction, even in their New Woman novels? By
addressing such questions, critics are able to provide a more complete
picture of the decade and the social and literary contribution women
writers made to it.

A good example of criticism that analyzes the writers in terms of the
threat they represented is an essay by Linda Dowling, "The Decadent
and the New Woman in the 1890's" (1979). Dowling reveals the fears
raised by the New Woman writers and their similarity to fears raised by
the decadents. Although the decadents and the New Woman writers are
today regarded as distinct, perhaps even antithetical, groups, Victorian
literary critics identified the New Woman with the decadent, since both
equally threatened established culture. Both expressed their "quarrel
with Victorian culture chiefly through sexual means—by heightening
sexual consciousness, candor, and expressiveness."[3] The New Woman, in
revolting against what was supposedly "natural," was perceived as a
threat to the culture and as allied with other forces of cultural anarchism, such as the decadents. Dowling notes that "in a cultural context
of radical anxiety, the decadent and the New Woman were twin apostles
of social apocalypse" (Dowling, 447). Dowling, like other recent critics,
believes that an evaluation of the backlash against these writers is requisite to an assessment of their place in literary history.

Criticism today has been useful in providing a social and historical
context for the literature of revolt and an explanation for its hostile
reception and subsequent marginalization. A recent critic, Marilyn
Bonnell (1993), in assessing Sarah Grand's *The Heavenly Twins* 100 years
after its publication, provides an explanation for the elimination of the
New Woman writers from the canon. Bonnell examines the fate of
Grand's novel, which sold in great numbers when it was published but
then received hostile criticism from male reviewers. Women writers of
the time, including Grand, were accused of failing to present a true picture of life because it did not conform to the reality that men found. The
literature of women was thus denegrated, and their novels marginalized.
Bonnell believes that "regardless of the feminine hold on the genre in
Grand's time" and "despite feminine literary ascendancy, the process of
canonization and marginalization erased an alternative version of the
New Woman illustrated by Sarah Grand" and other women of the time
(Bonnell, 472–73). Male critics of Grand's time, "the cultural power
brokers," as Bonnell calls them, "valorized the masculine conceptions of

the New Woman to the exclusion of those women writers so prevalent at the time" (Bonnell, 473). The great feminine influence on the novel was halted by denegrating women's work and "establishing the sovereignty of masculine viewpoint and knowledge" (Bonnell, 473).

In 1993, in her introduction to a collection of women's short stories of the 1890s, *Daughters of Decadence: Women Writers of the Fin-de-Siècle,* Showalter gives a much higher assessment of women writers of the decade and their importance to women's literary history than that which she gave in 1977, now claiming them to be a vital link between the earlier Victorian writers and those of this century:

> Their contributions to the evolution of women's writing, the fiction of the *fin de siècle,* and the genealogy of modernism have been neglected or forgotten. . . . They are the missing links between the great women writers of the Victorian novel and the modern fiction of Mansfield, Woolf, and Stein.[4]

In the last few years, partly because we are also in the last decade of a century with some parallel concerns of an earlier fin de siècle, there has been renewed interest in the 1890s, but most of the recent examination of the literature of the period has focused on the New Woman writers and the decadents. Much critical work still remains to be done, particularly on individual writers and on those who fall outside the category of New Woman writers, but not much progress can be made until more of the novels by women of the decade are reissued and thus become accessible to a wider group of students and scholars. A few presses, such as Virago and the Feminist Press, have published some of these novels by women in paperback, such as Mary Cholmondeley's *Red Pottage* (1985) and George Egerton's *Keynotes and Discords* (1983), while Grand's *The Heavenly Twins* was reissued by the University of Michigan Press in 1992. But many of the works have been out of print for a long time, some since the 1890s.

Nevertheless, the desire by feminists to recover lost and neglected women writers will undoubtedly lead to a continued examination of the contribution women writers made to the literary and social life of this decade and to the historical place they occupy in the development of the novel and short story. Their fiction should also be read and enjoyed for its variety of interesting and outspoken heroines, many of whom would feel quite at home among any group of feminists today.

Notes and References

Chapter One

1. See, for example, Hugh Stutfield, "The Psychology of Feminism," *Blackwood's* 161 (January 1897); hereafter cited in text. The phrase "doctrines of feminism" is used in a book review of *The Grasshoppers* in *Athenaeum* (27 April 1895): 533. Other, similar uses of "feminism" as well as "feminist" appear in the newspapers of the decade.

2. Elaine Showalter, *A Literature of Their Own: British Women Novelists from Brontë to Lessing* (Princeton, N.J.: Princeton University Press, 1977), 13; hereafter cited in text.

3. *"Keynotes," Critic* 24 (16 June 1894): 405; hereafter cited in text as *"Keynotes."*

4. "Some New Novels," *Spectator* (13 November 1897): 691–92; hereafter cited in text as "Some New."

5. "Recent Novels," *Nation* (16 November 1893): 374.

6. Numbers in parenthetical citations refer to pages.

7. "Recent Novels," *Spectator* (25 March 1893): 395; hereafter cited in text as "Recent Novels."

Chapter Two

1. Sarah Grand, "The New Aspect of the Woman Question," *North American Review* 158 (March 1894): 271; hereafter cited in text as "New Aspect."

2. Sarah Grand, *Ideala* (New York: Optimus Printing Company, 1894), 58; hereafter cited in text as *I.*

3. Sarah Grand, "The Man of the Moment," *North American Review* 158 (May 1894): 622; hereafter cited in text as "The Man."

4. Sarah Grand, *The Heavenly Twins* (Ann Arbor: University of Michigan Press, 1992), 219; hereafter cited in text as *HT.*

5. Sarah Grand, "Should Married Women Follow Professions?" *Young Woman* 7 (April 1899): 257; hereafter cited in text as "Should."

6. Sarah Grand, *The Beth Book* (New York: Dial Press, 1980), 400; hereafter cited in text as *BB.*

7. Gillian Kersley, *Darling Madame: Sarah Grand and Devoted Friend* (London: Virago, 1983), 110; hereafter cited in text.

8. John Sutherland, *The Stanford Guide to Victorian Fiction* (Stanford, Calif.: Stanford University Press, 1989), 258; hereafter cited in text.

9. George Egerton, "A Keynote to *Keynotes,"* in *Ten Contemporaries,*

John Gawsworth, ed. (London: Ernest Benn Limited, 1932), 58; hereafter cited in the text as "Keynote."

10. George Egerton, *Keynotes* in *Keynotes and Discords* (London: Virago Press, 1983), 184; hereafter cited in the text as *K.*

11. George Egerton, *Discords* in *Keynotes and Discords* (London: Virago Press, 1983), 194; hereafter cited in the text as *D.*

Chapter Three

1.   Mary Cholmondeley, *Red Pottage* (New York: Harper and Brothers, 1900), 157; hereafter cited in text at *RP.*

2.   Mabel Wotton, "The Fifth Edition," in *Daughters of Decadence: Women Writers of the Fin-de-Siècle,* Elaine Showalter, ed. (New Brunswick, N. J.: Rutgers University Press, 1993), 145; hereafter cited in text as "Fifth."

3.   Mona Caird, *The Daughters of Danaus* (New York: Feminist Press, 1989), 376; hereafter cited in the text as *DD.*

4.   "New Novels," *Athenaeum* (27 November 1897): 747.

5.   Quoted in Marilyn Bonnell, "The Legacy of Sarah Grand's *The Heavenly Twins*: A Review Essay," *English Literature in Transition, 1880–1920* 36 (1993): 474; hereafter cited in text.

6.   Hugh Stutfield, " 'Tommyrotics,' " *Blackwood's* 157 (June 1895): 836; hereafter cited in text.

7.   Janet Todd, ed., *British Women Writers: A Critical Reference Guide* (New York: Continuum, 1989), 140; hereafter cited in text.

8.   Lyn Pykett, *The "Improper" Feminine: The Women's Sensation Novel and the New Woman Writers* (New York: Routledge, 1992), 42; hereafter cited in text.

9.   Frank E. Huggett, *Victorian England as Seen by Punch* (London: Sidgwick & Jackson, 1978), 164.

10.   D. H. Hannigan, "Sex in Fiction," *Westminster Review* 143 (June 1895): 619; hereafter cited in text.

11.   "Men's Women in Fiction," *Westminster Review* 149 (May 1898): 577.

12.   Mona Caird [first published under name G. Noel Hatton], *Whom Nature Leadeth* (London: Longmans, Green, and Company, 1883), 189; hereafter cited as *WNL.*

Chapter Four

1.   Mona Caird, "Marriage," *Westminster Review* 130 (August 1888): 197; hereafter cited in text as "Marriage."

2.   Gail Cunningham, *The New Woman and the Victorian Novel* (New York: Harper and Row, 1978), 63; hereafter cited in text.

3.   Millicent Fawcett, "The Woman Who Did," *Contemporary Review* 67 (May 1895): 629–630; hereafter cited in text.

4. Iota, *A Yellow Aster* (New York: George Munro's Sons, 1895), 73; hereafter cited in text as *YA.*

5. "Two 'New' Women," *Critic* (26 May 1894): 354.

6. Holbrook Jackson, *The Eighteen Nineties* (New York: Alfred A. Knopf, 1925), 46.

7. David Rubinstein, *Before the Suffragettes: Women's Emancipation in the 1890s* (New York: St. Martin's Press, 1986), 12; hereafter cited in text.

8. Ella Hepworth Dixon, *The Story of a Modern Woman* (London: Merlin Press, 1990), 13; hereafter cited in text as *Story.*

9. Menie Muriel Dowie, *Gallia* (London: Methuen & Co., 1895), 65; hereafter cited in text as *G.*

10. Emma Frances Brooke, *A Superfluous Woman* [published anonymously] (New York: Cassell, 1894), 11; hereafter cited in text as *SW.*

11. Elaine Showalter, *Sexual Anarchy: Gender and Culture at the Fin de Siècle* (New York: Viking Penguin, 1990), 198.

12. Norman and Jeanne Mackenzie, *The Fabians* (New York: Simon and Schuster, 1977), 64.

13. Emma Frances Brooke, *Transition* ["By the Author of *A Superfluous Woman*"] (Philadelphia: J. B. Lippincott, 1895), 326; hereafter cited in text as *T.*

Chapter Five

1. Adeline Sergeant, *The Story of a Penitent Soul* (New York: Lovell, Coryell and Company, 1892), 272; hereafter cited in text as *Soul.*

2. John Oliver Hobbes, *The School for Saints* (London: T. Fisher Unwin, 1897), 96; hereafter cited in text as *School.*

3. George Moore, *Celibates* (New York: Macmillan and Co., 1895), 254.

Chapter Six

1. Lee's historical studies include *Studies of the Eighteenth Century in Italy* (1880) and *Renaissance Fancies and Studies* (1895); her books on aesthetics include *The Handling of Words* (1923) and *Music and its Lovers* (1933); her travel books include *Genius Loci* (1899), *The Spirit of Rome* (1906), and *The Sentimental Traveller* (1908); and her plays include *Ariadne in Mantua* (1903) and *The Ballet of the Nations* (1915).

2. Peter Gunn, *Vernon Lee: Violet Paget, 1856–1935* (London: Oxford University Press, 1964), 129; hereafter cited in text.

3. Vernon Lee, *Hauntings: Fantastic Stories* (Freeport, New York: Books for Libraries Press, 1971), 53; hereafter cited in text as *H.*

4. Gunn quotes from a letter James sent to Lee about *Miss Brown*: " 'The imperfection of the book seems to me to reside (apart from, occasionally, a kind of intellectualized rowdyism of style) in a certain ferocity . . . you take the aesthetic business too seriously, too tragically, and above all with

too great an implication of sexual motives . . . you have impregnated all those people too much with the sexual, the basely erotic preoccupation' " (quoted in Gunn [his ellipses], 104–05). See Gunn, pp. 103–07, for a more complete discussion of James's reaction to the novel.

5. Vernon Lee, *Vanitas: Polite Stories* (London: William Heinemann, 1892), 53; hereafter cited in text as *V*.

Chapter Seven

1. Ella D'Arcy, "Irremediable," *Yellow Book* I (April 1894), 88; hereafter all stories from the *Yellow Book* will be cited in text as *YB* followed by the volume number.

Chapter Eight

1. A. R. Cunningham, "The 'New Woman Fiction' of the 1890's," *Victorian Studies* 17 (December 1973): 186.

2. Patricia Stubbs, *Women and Fiction: Feminism and the Novel 1880–1920* (Sussex, England: Harvester Press, 1979), 117–118; hereafter cited in text.

3. Linda Dowling, "The Decadent and the New Woman in the 1890's," *Nineteenth Century Fiction* 33 (1979): 441; hereafter cited in text.

4. Elaine Showalter, ed., *Daughters of Decadence: Women Writers of the Fin de Siècle* (New Brunswick, N. J.:Rutgers University Press, 1993), viii.

Bibliography

Primary Sources
The first British edition of each book is listed. If there is a recent edition of a novel, publication information is given subsequently.

Allen, Grant. *The Woman Who Did*. London: John Lane, 1895.

Brooke, Emma Frances. *A Superfluous Woman*. 3 vols. London: W. Heinemann, 1894.

————. *Transition*. ["By the author of *A Superfluous Woman*"] London: W. Heinemann, 1895.

Caird, Mona. *The Daughters of Danaus*. London: Sands & Co, 1894; New York: Feminist Press, 1989.

————. "Marriage." *Westminster Review* 130 (August 1888): 186–201.

————. *Whom Nature Leadeth*. [Published under the name G. Noel Hatton]. 3 vols. London: Longmans, Green, and Company, 1883.

Cholmondeley, Mary. *Red Pottage*. London: Edward Arnold, 1899; New York, New York: Penguin Books–Virago Press, 1985.

Cross, Victoria [Vivian Cory]. "Theodora, a Fragment." *Yellow Book* IV (January 1895). 156–88.

D'Arcy, Ella. "At Twickenham." *Yellow Book* XII (January 1897): 313–32.

————. "Irremediable." *Yellow Book* I (April 1894): 87–108.

————. "A Marriage." *Yellow Book* XI (October 1896): 309–42.

————. *Monochromes*. London: John Lane, 1895.

————. "The Pleasure-Pilgrim." *Yellow Book* V (April 1895): 34–67.

————. "Poor Cousin Louis." *Yellow Book* II (July 1894): 34–59.

————. "Sir Julian Garve." *Yellow Book* XIII (April 1897): 291–307.

————. "Two Stories." *Yellow Book* X (July 1896): 265–85.

————. "The Web of Maya." *Yellow Book* VII (October 1895): 291–318.

————. "White Magic." *Yellow Book* III (October 1894): 59–68.

Dixon, Ella Hepworth. *The Story of a Modern Woman*. London: W. Heinemann, 1894; London: Merlin Press, 1990.

————. "The Sweet o' the Year." *Yellow Book* IX (April 1896): 158–63.

Dixon, Marion Hepworth. "A Thief in the Night." *Yellow Book* IV (January 1895): 239–46.

Dowie, Menie Muriel. *Gallia*. London: Methuen & Co, 1895.

————. "An Idyll in Millinery." *Yellow Book* X (July 1896): 24–53.

Egerton, George. "The Captain's Book." *Yellow Book* VI (July 1895): 103–16.

————. *Discords*. London: J. Lane, 1894.

————. *Keynotes*. London: E. Mathews & J. Lane, 1893.

————. *Keynotes and Discords*. London: Virago Press, 1983.

————. "A Keynote to *Keynotes*," in *Ten Contemporaries,* John Gawsworth, ed. London: Ernest Benn Limited, 1932.

————. "A Lost Masterpiece." *Yellow Book* I (April 1894): 189–96.

Gissing, George. *The Odd Women.* London: Lawrence & Bullen, 1893; New York: Penguin Books, 1983.

Grand, Sarah. *The Beth Book.* London: W. Heinemann, 1898; New York: Dial Press, 1980.

————. *The Heavenly Twins.* 3 vol. London: W. Heinemann, 1893; Ann Arbor: University of Michigan Press, 1992.

————. *Ideala.* London: E. W. Allen, 1888; New York: Optimus Printing Company, 1894.

————. "The Man of the Moment." *North American Review* 158 (May 1894): 620–27.

————. "The New Aspect of the Woman Question." *North American Review* 158 (March 1894): 270–76.

————. "Should Married Women Follow Professions?" *Young Woman* 7 (April 1899): 257–59.

Hickson, Mrs. Murray [Mabel Kitcat]. "Martha." *Yellow Book* VII (October 1895): 267–79.

Hobbes, John Oliver. *The School for Saints.* London: T. F. Unwin, 1897.

Iota. *A Yellow Aster.* London: Hutchinson & Co., 1894.

Lee, Vernon. *Hauntings: Fantastic Stories.* London: W. Heinemann, 1890; Freeport, New York: Books for Libraries Press, 1971.

————. "Prince Alberic and the Snake Lady." *Yellow Book* X (July 1896): 289–344.

————. *Vanitas: Polite Stories.* London: W. Heinemann, 1892.

Leverson, Mrs. Ernest [Ada]. "Suggestion." *Yellow Book* V (April 1895): 249–57.

————. "The Quest for Sorrow." *Yellow Book* VIII (January 1896): 325–35.

Macdonald, Leila. "Jeanne-Marie." *Yellow Book* III (October 1894): 215–40.

Mew, Charlotte. "Passed." *Yellow Book* II (July 1894): 121–41.

Milman, Lena. "Marcel: an Hotel-Child." *Yellow Book* XII (January 1897): 141–64.

Moore, George. *Celibates.* London: Walter Scott, 1895.

Radford, Ada. "Lot 99." *Yellow Book* XI (October 1896): 267–82.

————. "Lucy Wren." *Yellow Book* XIII (April 1897): 272–84.

Sergeant, Adeline. *The Story of a Penitent Soul.* New York: Lovell, Coryell & Company, 1892. [First American edition]

Sharp, Evelyn. "The Other Anna." *Yellow Book* XIII (April 1897): 170–93.

————. "The Restless River." *Yellow Book* XII (January 1897): 167–87.

Showalter, Elaine, ed. *Daughters of Decadence: Women Writers of the Fin-de-Siècle.* New Brunswick, N.J.: Rutgers University Press, 1993. A collection of British and American short stories by women writers from the 1890s.

Syrett, Netta. "Far Above Rubies." *Yellow Book* XII (January 1897): 250–72.
————. "Thy Heart's Desire." *Yellow Book* II (July 1894): 228–55.
Wotton, Mabel. *Day-Books*. London: John Lane, 1896.

Secondary Sources

1. Books

Ardis, Ann L. *New Women, New Novels: Feminism and Early Modernism*. New Brunswick, N.J., and London: Rutgers University Press, 1990. Fine analysis of the New Woman novels and their challenge to the dominant Victorian ideology.

Casford, Ethel Lenore. *The Magazines of the 1890s*. Language and Literature Series Vol. 1, No. 1. Eugene, Ore.: University Press, Sept. 1929. Brief but useful description of the various literary periodicals of the 1890s.

Cunningham, Gail. *The New Woman and the Victorian Novel*. New York: Harper & Row, 1978. Mostly on the New Woman as depicted by male writers but a good chapter on women writers.

Flint, Kate. Introduction to *The Story of a Modern Woman*. London: Merlin Press, 1990. Some biographical information about Ella Hepworth Dixon and a valuable discussion of the novel.

Gunn, Peter. *Vernon Lee: Violet Paget, 1856–1935*. London: Oxford University Press, 1964. Detailed and informative biography of Lee combined with discussions of her many literary works.

Harrison, Fraser, ed. *The Yellow Book: An Illustrated Quarterly*. London: Sidgwick and Jackson, 1974. Good introduction to the publication background of the *Yellow Book* and reasons for its demise.

Huggett, Frank E. *Victorian England as seen by Punch*. London: Sidgwick & Jackson, 1978. Excerpts from the journal over the years with an informative discussion; includes many cartoons from *Punch*.

Jackson, Holbrook. *The Eighteen Nineties*. New York: Alfred A. Knopf, 1925. Important early critical book on the 1890s, with an emphasis on the decadents.

Kersley, Gillian. *Darling Madame: Sarah Grand and Devoted Friend*. London: Virago, 1983. Only biography of Grand, with detailed information on the publication history of her novels.

Mackenzie, Norman, and Jeanne Mackenzie. *The Fabians*. New York: Simon & Schuster, 1977. Informative book on the Fabian circle which included many women; Emma Brooke was one.

Mix, Katherine Lyon. *A Study in Yellow: The Yellow Book and its Contributors*. Lawrence: University of Kansas Press, 1960. Detailed discussion of the many people associated with the literary journal.

Pykett, Lyn. *The 'Improper' Feminine: The Women's Sensation Novel and the New Woman Writing*. London and New York: Routledge, 1992. Explains

Victorian anxieties created by sensation novels of the 1860s and the New Woman fiction of the 1890s.

Rubinstein, David. *Before the Suffragettes: Women's Emancipation in the 1890s.* New York: St. Martin's Press, 1986. Literary achievement of the New Woman writers put in the context of women's emancipation during the 1890s.

Shattock, Joanne. *The Oxford Guide to British Woman Writers.* Oxford: Oxford University Press, 1993. Valuable reference book, combining short biographies with literary works.

Showalter, Elaine. *A Literature of Their Own: British Women Novelists From Brontë to Lessing.* Princeton, N. J.: Princeton University Press, 1993. A significant work for recovering many forgotten women writers; puts their fiction into the context of the development of the novel.

————. *Sexual Anarchy: Gender and Culture at the Fin de Siècle.* New York: Viking Penguin, 1990. Excellent study of gender issues in the 1890s; an interesting chapter on the New Woman.

Stubbs, Patricia. *Women and Fiction: Feminism and the Novel 1880–1920.* Sussex, England: Harvester Press, 1979. Good discussion of both men and women writers of the period with chapters on the short story and feminist fiction.

Sutherland, John. *The Stanford Companion to Victorian Fiction.* Palo Alto, Calif.: Stanford University Press, 1989. Indispensable reference book on Victorian fiction, containing biographical information and plot summaries.

Todd, Janet, ed. *British Women Writers: A Critical Reference Guide.* New York: Continuum, 1989. Short biographies of women writers with some bibliographic material.

Vicinus, Martha. Introduction to *Keynotes and Discords.* London: Virago Press, 1983. Good discussion of Egerton's importance as a writer.

White, Terence de Vere. *A Leaf from The Yellow Book.* London: Richards Press, 1958. Combines biography, diary entries, letters, and personal memories of George Egerton by White, the son of Egerton's cousin.

2. Contemporary Journal Articles

Fawcett, Millicent. "The Woman Who Did." *Contemporary Review* 67 (May 1895): 625–31. Scathing review of Grant Allen's novel.

Hannigan, D. H. "Sex in Fiction." *Westminster Review* 143 (June 1895): 616–25. Defends use of sex in fiction but cites only novels by male writers for his examples.

"Keynotes." *Critic* 24 (16 June 1894): 405. Review of Egerton's *Keynotes* that is highly critical: too much sex and too little artistry.

"Men's Women in Fiction." *Westminster Review* 149 (May 1898): 571–77. Complains about the way women are depicted in men's fiction, concluding that men do not know women at all.

"New Novels." *Athenaeum.* 27 November 1897: 743–44. Harsh review of Grand's *The Beth Book.*

"Recent Novels." *Spectator.* 25 March 1893, 395. Review condemns Grand's *The Heavenly Twins* for its polemics and lack of form.

"Some New Novels." *Spectator.* 13 November 1897: 690–93. Harsh review of Grand's *The Beth Book,* claiming it is not a novel but part of the author's "sex-crusade."

Stutfield, Hugh. "The Psychology of Feminism." *Blackwood's* 161 (January 1897): 104–17. Attack on New Women as writers of "neurotic fiction."

———. "Tommyrotics." *Blackwood's* 157 (June 1895): 833–45. New Woman writers accused of being "erotomaniacs," writing "morbid and nasty books."

"Two 'New' Women," *Critic* (26 May 1894): 353–54. A critical attack on Iota's *A Yellow Aster.*

"The Yoke of the Virgin." *Nation* 58 (17 May 1894): 369–70. A review of *A Yellow Aster* turns into a denunciation of recent novels for their indecency.

3. Modern Critical Essays

Bonnell, Marilyn. "The Legacy of Sarah Grand's *The Heavenly Twins*: A Review Essay." *English Literature in Transition, 1880–1920* 36 (1993): 467–78. Brief discussion of Grand's novel and its relationship to other New Woman fiction.

Cunningham. A. R. "The 'New Woman Fiction' of the 1890's." *Victorian Studies* 17 (December 1973): 177–86. One of the first essays to appear on the New Woman writers; distinguishes two types of New Woman fiction.

Dowling, Linda. "The Decadent and the New Woman in the 1890s." *Nineteenth Century Fiction* 33 (1979): 434–53. Excellent discussion of the differences between decadent and New Woman writers, revealing the public fears both groups unleashed.

Stetz, Margaret. "Turning Points: Mabel E. Wotton." *Turn-of-the-Century Women* III (Winter 1986): 2–3. Finds in Wotton's career and fiction clues to the demise of women's fiction of the 1890s.

Index

The Author

Carolyn Christensen Nelson is a member of the English Department at West Virginia University. Her Ph.D. from the University of Wisconsin is in Victorian literature. She has written the entries on Sarah Grand and Mona Caird for the *Dictionary of Literary Biography* and published an article on the religious implications of novels by Victorian women in the *Midwest Quarterly* (Spring 1994). She has also published an article on representations of Helen in Greek mythology.